Mrs. Ethel Baker Callis
29 S. State St.-Apt. 801
Salt Lake City, Utah 84111

BX
8670.1
.B178b
1910

MORMON AMERICANA

HAROLD B. LEE LIBRARY
Brigham Young University
Americana Collection

3 1197 23318 5708

COAT OF ARMS—BAKER FAMILY, ESSEX, ENGLAND.
A Griffin—Passant—Vert.

AMENZO WHITE BAKER, Sr., 120

THE
BAKER GENEALOGY

AND

COLLATERAL BRANCHES

BY
AMENZO WHITE BAKER
OF MENDON, UTAH

REVISED AND PUBLISHED BY MERLIN J. STONE

OGDEN UTAH
A. T. HESTMARK
Printer

EDITOR'S PREFACE

It is proper to state here that as the author, Amenzo White Baker, now deceased, did not live to oversee the labors of publishing his genealogical collections, this duty was entrusted to the writer, with instructions to revise the same, to compile and add thereto the records of all the descendants of Simon Baker, one of Utah's pioneers, as may be procured in time for publication, together with the liberal privilege of editor.

I wish also to add my testimony that the author was indefatigable in collecting the records of these families, and that all the descendants of the Puritan Ancestor whose genealogy has been traced in this book have reason to congratulate .themselves in the fidelity with which he has executed his work.

Ogden, Utah, A. D. 1910.   MERLIN J. STONE.

INTRODUCTORY

The object of this Baker record is to collect the various and fragmentary records of the descendants of Rev. Thomas Baker, who came to America about 1650 from Dedham, Essex, England, and settled in Rhode Island, that the present and future generations may have better knowledge of their relations, one to the other, and that the links connecting us with our worthy sires, the Pilgrim Fathers, may not disappear altogether. With this in view, the compiler has spent many hours in correspondence, in personal interviews with many individuals of the Baker family, has listened to many a detail of family history, and has made such selections as should be preserved.

He took great pleasure in entrusting these records to his nephew, Albert Mowry Baker, Jr., with instructions to keep them sacred, and add thereto records of all descendants that should be presented, and that at some future time the genealogy might be completed and published.

Mr. A. M. Baker, Jr., worthy of the trust of the compiler, having kept the record sacred and intact from 1892 until June 15, 1909, not being in a position to give the work the necessary attention of a revision, through the advice and counsel of his father and aunt, Betsie Topham, the work was delivered to the writer to revise. The records compiled by Amenzo W. Baker, consisting of nearly all the records in this volume from the Rev. Thomas Baker, our English progenitor, down to Simon Baker, and on the receipt of the revised work—in typewritten form—December 13, 1909, through consultation with a number of the Bakers, it was decided to have the writer compile and add thereto the records of Simon Baker and his descendants, and publish the same, under the direction of Geo. W. Baker, Sr., Joseph Baker and A. M. Baker, Jr., as the Baker Genealogical Committee.

As a race the Bakers are intellectual and educated, and while they are somewhat reserved in manner and averse to much demonstration of feeling, they may be said to be genuine and honest, endowed with their full share of independence of thought and action, with tenacity of purpose (sometimes to obstinacy), fidelity to one another and to their country, and a high sense of honor, with a respect and reverence for the religion of their forefathers, while the most of them have manifested a spirit of deep and earnest piety.

Many of them have been graduates from our colleges and seminaries, and have filled posts of honor and usefulness; while others, without a college education, have served their country and generation faithfully.

The family have reason to feel proud, that among its members were the diplomatist, the journalist, the soldier, the statesman, the teacher, the divine, the missionary, the literateur, the dramatist, the physician, the manufacturer, the jurist, the inventor, the scientist, in short, no profession or department could be mentioned that is not graced and dignified by some one of our family.

We, therefore, may recall these facts, not in a spirit of vain glory, but as furnishing reasons for our recording the history of our ancestors. Sancho Panzo remarked: "Blessed is the man who has a father"; but there are none of us but can go back not only to our own father, but to his great-great-great-grandfather, how much more blessed are we than the squire of the renowned and redoubtable, Don Quixote!

Having an eminent ancestor will make the descendant ambitious to make himself worthy of his descent. Hence, a noble ancestry—not of wealth necessarily, but of deeds—tends to make its descendants anxious to emulate the virtues of their predecessors.

One of our sweetest and most delightful bards has sung:

> "Lives of great men all remind us,
> We can make our lives sublime,
> And, departing, leave behind us,
> Footprints in the sands of time."

And if this is true regarding the lives of great men in nowise related to us, how much more does the above sentiment of Longfellow apply to those of the Baker family, who know that many of these whose lives are so "sublime" belong to their own individual ancestors.

After an extensive research among the different branches of the family, we take pleasure in adding that no traitor to his country has been found among them, and that we need not be ashamed of the name that has been handed down to us, and which marks among the earliest of our beloved land such men as the Rev. Thomas Baker, guided by high and noble principle, whose allegiance was to the triune God, who dared the perils of the sea and life on a rocky, desolate coast, because the love of liberty in religion and government, demanded a fresher atmosphere than old England extended to them.

To all who have rendered assistance in contributing data and other information, we would return many thanks. If others who have been addressed had taken interest in the work, and contributed concerning their branches, our genealogical tree would have been more fully leaved; but with its imperfections, let the present generation of Bakers receive it, at the hand of the willing writer.

M. J. S.

CONTENTS

Part First: Thomas Baker (1) and his descendants of the Baker name, numbered and arranged in consecutive order.

Where the name is followed by (X), it denotes, of whom hereafter. The record of such person may be found under that number in its record order.

Part Second: Record of the Baker daughters and their descendants.

Part Third: Collateral branches arranged in the following order:
The Hill Family.
The Leavitt Family.
The Mowry Family.
The Richards Family.
The Shepardson Lineage.
The Sherman Lineage.
The Shumway Family.
The Staples Family.
The Stillman Lineage.
The Stone Lineage.
The Thorn Lineage.
The Young Family.

If any errors or omissions are discovered, or if any additional facts are learned, or new branches of the family are heard from, write the information as completely as possible, and send for insertion in succeeding volumes to A. M. Baker, Mendon, Utah.

While there are but few volumes of the Baker Genealogy in excess of the number subscribed for, these may be secured, while they last, by communicating with Merlin J. Stone, at Ogden, Utah.

In addition to the Ancestral and Collateral branches of the Baker families as collected together by Amenzo W. Baker, the records of all the descendants of Simon Baker to April 15, 1910, were compiled by Merlin J. Stone, with the generous assistance of the Baker Committee.

These records were collected through correspondence with the families during three months time, a remarkable collection, considering that they cover this whole western country from Wyoming to the coast and from Canada to Old Mexico.

The descendants of Simon Baker were as follows:

Children	Males	12	females	12	Total	24
Grandchildren	Males	80	females	90	Total	170
Great-grandchildren	Males	116	females	119	Total	235
Great-great-grandchildren	Males	5	females	2	Total	7
Grand total		213		223		436

PART FIRST

Thomas Baker and His Descendants of the Baker Name.

(1)

THOMAS BAKER, the earliest of the name to which we trace, was born 1638 at Dedham, Essex, England, and came early to America and settled on Rhode Island. December 17, 1653, the land of Thomas Baker is mentioned as adjoining that of George Kenrick of Newport, R. I., in a deed of the latter to William Field of Providence.

The church records of the First Baptist Church of Newport, of which he was a member, show that he was ordained in 1655. In 1656 he and William Vaughn and others left the First Baptist Church of Newport, and established the Second Baptist Church. He was made pastor. The reasons given for this separation are thus stated: "Said persons conceived a prejudice against Psalmody and against the restraints that the liberty of Prophesying was laid under and also against the doctrine of particular redemption and against the rite of laying on of hands, as a matter of indifference." In 1666 he removed to Kingston, and gathered a church together, of which he became its first pastor(officiating for many years in that capacity, his successor, Wm. Sweet, following in 1710. He married Sarah ———. See Austin's General History of R. I.

Children:

2 Thomas,   X
3 Benjamin, b. 1676.   X
4 James.   X

Thomas Baker (1) was a tailor by trade, always signing deeds, etc., after he had been many years a minister, "Thomas Baker, Tailor."

(2)

THOMAS BAKER was born at Newport, R. I., where he married Mary ———. In his will, made Feb. 20, 1743, he mentions all his children except Joshua, Joseph and Ruth, who probably died before. May 27, 1729, Thomas and five others bought 79 acres of the vacant lands in Naragansett. Executor Jeremiah gave Thomas £50, John 5s, Abner £40, Josiah 5s, Philip £45, Ichabod £5; daughter Sarah ———— and Elizabeth Greene all household goods, Anna 5s, Jeremiah homestead buildings.

Children:
5 Thomas, b. Jan. 7, 169--
6 John, b. Sept. 20, 1699.
7 Jeremiah, b. July 26, 170--
8 Abner, b. Mar. 6, 170--
9 Sarah, b. Dec. 15, 170--
10 Josiah, b. Oct. 11, 170--
11 Joshua, b. Feb. 11, 170--
12 Joseph, b. Feb. 17, 17--
13 Elizabeth, m. —— Greene.
14 Ann, m. April 9, 1732, Daniel Austin, second, Stephen Sweet; he d. 1737.
15 Philip.
16 Ruth.
17 Ichabod.

(3)

BENJAMIN BAKER was born 1676 at Kingston, R. I., and married there Mary H————.

Children: Born at West Kingston.
18 Benjamin, b. 1698. X

(4)

JAMES BAKER was born at Newport, R. I., where he married Penelope, daughter of Amos and Deborah (Stafford), Westcott.
Children:
19 A daughter, name cannot be made out.
20 Daniel,
21 Abel,
22 George,
23 Alice.

(18)

BENJAMIN BAKER was born at West Kingston, R. I., 1698. Died there about 1730. May 27, 1729, Benjamin Baker and twelve others bought 1,824 acres near Devil's Foot. These all lived at Kingston.

Children: Born at North Kingston.
24 Benjamin, b. 1720. X
25 Mercy, m. Geo. Hawley in R. I.

(24)

BENJAMIN BAKER was born 1720 at North Kingston, where he married first, Mary, daughter of Elisha Sherman. (See Sherman lineage). He married second, Mary Potter.

Children:
26 Benjamin, b. June 27, 1750.
27 Elijah, m. Martha ————. X.

28 Jirah, b. Jan. 28, 1764, m. Mary, dau. of Increase Moseley. X
29 John, m. Sarah ———.
30 Noah, m. Polly ———. Settled in Hoosick, N. Y.
31 Mercy, m. George Hawley.
32 Mary (Polly), m. Clark Babcock.
33 Sherman, m. first Mary ———, second Sarah ———. X.
34 Sarah, m. Benj. Harrington.
35 Lydia, m. Samuel Scribner.
36 Norman, d. unm. when a young man.
37 Thomas Potter, m. Mary Tanner. X

(26)

DEACON BENJAMIN BAKER was born June 27, 1750, at South Kingston, R. I., and died September 28, 1828, at Leydon, Mass. He married first, Lois, a daughter of Oliver and Patience Babcock, who was born 1754, at South Kingston, R. I. He married second, Hannah Tucker, who was born 1754 at South Kingston, R. I. He married third, Mary Babcock, sister to his first wife. She was born 1758 at South Kingston.

He was a shoemaker and a farmer. His neighbors used to work for him on his farm for shoemaking and mending. An upright man whom everybody believed in implicitly, apt to be chosen when any matter was to be arbitrated. Very unassuming and retiring, he was averse to attracting attention. He was a member of the Baptist Church, and always called "Deacon Baker." He was a militia man a short time. Was in the Revolutionary war. Came from Rhode Island to Leydon about 1777. The country at Leydon was unimproved, and all woods.

The following inscriptions were copied from headstones in West Leydon Cemetery by William H. Shepardson, during a visit there in September, 1887. Finding Deacon Benjamin's headstone broken down and in four or five pieces, he replaced it with a new one, and had the same inscription placed thereon.

"Deacon Benjamin Baker died September 28, 1828, A. E. 78.

> The sweet remembrance of the just
> Shall flourish when their forms are dust."

"Mrs. Hannah, wife of Deacon Benjamin Baker, died Nov. 2, 1805, A. E. 51.

> The liveliest virtues of the mind
> And body, were in her combined,
> No pencil can her virtues paint
> She lived a Christian, died a saint."

"Mary, relict of Dea. Benjamin Baker, died Nov. 2, 1843, aged 83." Mrs. Hannah (Tucker) Baker had a brother Newman, who was a great penman. He wrote her family record in her Bible.

Children: Born at Leydon, Mass.

37½ A child by first wife, d. aged 3 or 4 years.

    Children by second wife:
38 Jesse, b. Jan. 1778, lived in Hoosick. X
39 Benjamin, b. Oct. 26, 1780. X
40 Newman, b. Jan. 26, 1783, lived in Hoosick. X
41 Lucy, b. Oct. 12, 1785, died a young woman. Twin.
42 Lois, b. Oct. 12, 1785, died a few months old. Twin.
43 Jirah, b. April 18, 1788. X
44 Simon Clark, b. Oct. 11, 1790, m. Roxana Patterson. X
45 Hannah, b. Feb. 19, 1793, m. Randall Miner. X
46 Mary, b. Aug. 7, 1795, m. William Henry Shepardson. X

(27)

ELIJAH BAKER was born at South Kingston, R. I., came with his parents to Leydon, where he lived for a number of years, and later in different places in York State and several different places in Ohio. The last heard of him he was living with his son-in-law, James Avery, in Medina County, Ohio, where he no doubt died. He married Martha ———.

    Children:
47 Mercy.
48 Junia, lived at Fairfield Center, Huron County, Ohio; had large family.
49 Jirah, had large family.

(28)

JIRAH BAKER was born January 28, 1764, at Kingston, R. I. He was a farmer and settled in Hoosick, N. Y., where he was Justice of the Peace for many years and filled many of the town offices, and was a most estimable and worthy citizen. He married in 1792 at Hoosick, N. Y., Mary, daughter of Increase Mosely. (See Hyde Gen., page 645.) She was born April 6, 1777, at Belchertown, and died November 3, 1827, at Hoosick, N. Y. He died June 4, 1846.

    Children: Born in Hoosick.
50 Lucina, b. April 19, 1794, d. Jan. 11, 1796.
51 Clark, b. March 3, 1796, m. Lucina Welch. X
52 Jonathan, b. Nov. 6, 1797, m. Sarah Chapman. X
53 Norman, b. Oct. 27, 1799, m. Waity Gibbs. X
54 Esther, b. Oct. 20, 1801, m. John Brown. X
55 Sidney, b. Sept. 14, 1803, d. Dec. 2, 1804.
56 Mary, b. May 17, 1805, m. Arunah Mosely. X
57 Increase, b. July 21, 1807, m. Julia A. Canfield. X
58 Jirah Eaton, b. June, 1810, m. Elmira Gifford. X

(29)

JOHN BAKER was born at South Kingston, R. I. Removed

when young to Leydon, Mass. He married Sarah —— and settled in Hoosick, N. Y., where he raised a large family.

Children:
59 Samuel.

(32)

SHERMAN BAKER was born at South Kingston, R. I., and came with his parents while a child to Leydon, Mass. He married first Mary —— and second Sarah —— and settled in Hoosick, N. Y. He was a well built man, six feet tall, large frame. He had seven sons and three daughters.

Children:
60 Lathen, b. Oct. 28, 1796, living in April 23, 1886.
61 Thomas, b. February, 1800, living in April 23, 1886.
The eight others died previous to 1886.

(37)

THOMAS POTTER BAKER was born ——, married Mary Tanner, who was born March 10, 1776. He died September, 1825.

Children:
62 Benjamin, b. March 26, 1796, m. February, 1821, Abigal Kruyer Taylor. X
63 Thankful, b. 1798, m. Elijah Ferguson. X
64 Joshua, b. 1800, m. Catherine Bonner. Had 6 children. He died young. Three of his children died young.
65 Jirah. Never married.
66 Clark Carrington.
67 Iram, m. Dorcas Olds, d. 3 months later.
68 Susan, d. while young.
69 Mehitable, b. March 26, 1812, m. Geo. Terry.
70 A daughter, d. three weeks old.
71 Eunice, d. while a young woman.
72 Eliza, m. Mr. Hoyt.
73 William, b. December, 1824.

(38)

JESSE BAKER was born Jan. 23, 1778, at Leydon, Mass. Went to Western New York, where he married his first wife, and later moved to Illinois. He afterwards married again and then lived in Hoosick, N. Y., until he came to Ohio in 1835. He was a shoemaker, and also a doctor of the Thompsonian System. Second wife died in the fall of 1846, in Mills County, Iowa. He died during the winter of 1847, in Mills County, Iowa. He joined the Latter-day Saints Church and was noted for his faith and zeal in the ordinances of the gospel.

Children:
74 Mary, b. Feb. 10, 1801, d. March 24, 1872, m. Carey Burdick. X

REBECCA (THORN) BAKER 39

(39)

BENJAMIN BAKER was born Oct. 26, 1780, at Leydon, Mass., and died Feb. 5, 1857, at Unadilla Forks, Oswego County, New York. He married Rebacca, daughter of Henry and Prudence (Noyes) Thorn. (See Thorn lineage.) She was born May 12, 1786. Died May 31, 1872.

Children: Born at West Winfield.
75 Hannah, b. 1806, d. Nov. 25, 1851, m. Edwin Waters. X
76 Mary, b. Nov. 12, 1807, d. Aug. 21, 1874, m. Eli W. Miner. X
77 Simon, b. Oct. 18, 1811, d. Oct. 22, 1863. X
78 Aurilla, b. April 10, 1815, d. Oct. 10, 1836. Single.
79 Samuel, b. Dec. 7, 1817, d. June 9, 1819.

(40)

NEWMAN BAKER was born Jan. 26, 1783, at Leydon, Mass. Lived at Hoosick, N. Y., and left there and was killed by the Indians while chopping in the woods.

Children:
80 Jirah. Lived near Syracuse, but moved.

(43)

JIRAH BAKER was born April 18, 1787, at Leydon, Mass., and died at the home of his daughter, Mary A., April 16, 1877, at Clay, Onandaga County, New York. He married in 1814 at Union Village, Onandaga County, New York, Sarah Birge. She was born May 8, 1798, in Connecticut. After the death of her father, she being in her sixteenth year at the time of marriage, moved to her sister in Washington County, New York. Their first home was in the town of Lisander, while it was yet a wilderness, where they suffered all the ills of frontier life. They both were devoted students of the blessed word of God. She was a heroic woman and did good service in pleading for primitive Christianity, a good wife, a good mother, her long life, and kind deeds, will be locked up in the hearts of those who knew her best. She died at the home of her daughter, Mary Loomis, Feb. 25, 1871, at Clay, N. Y. In 1840 Mr. Baker and all his family, except Mary A., removed to Michigan and later removed in 1868 to his daughter's residence at Clay, N. Y., where he spent the remainder of his days, and where he was buried on his 90th birthday.

Children:
81 Horace F., b. in Lisander, N. Y., m. and lived in Tennessee.
82 Mary A., b. 1820, in Lisander, N. Y., m. Edward Loomis. X
83 Sarah Jane, b. May 18, 1822, at Clay, N. Y., m. John McKelvey. X

SIMON CLARK BAKER 44
(44)

SIMON CLARK BAKER was born Oct. 9, 1790, at Leydon, Mass. He married Roxana Patterson. He died April 20, 1867. She was the daughter of Dr. Eleazer and Dinah (Stanhope) Patterson, born Aug. 9, 1783, at Burlington, Otsego County, New York, and died June 16, 1866, at Marielle, town of Marcellus, Onandaga, N. Y.

Children: Born at Spafford, N. Y.
84 Mamie K., b. July 1, 1815, d. Oct. 31, 1884, m. Sept. 20, 1838, Reuben Smith. X
85 Emily B., b. May 2, 1817, d. July 6, 1873, m. Sept. 20, 1838, Amasa Sepions.
86 Roswell P., b. Nov. 7, 1818, d. Dec. 22, 1869, m. Elizabeth ——. X
87 Ashbell S., b. Nov. 3, 1820, d. Dec. 25, 1849. X
88 Roxana E., b. Sept. 21, 1822, m. Charles E. Rathbun, living April 6, 1891. X
89 Marquis, b. Dec. 27, 1824, d. Dec. 6, 1890. X
90 Calvin P., b. Sept. 9, 1827, d. Jan. 1, 1873, um.
91 Philetus, b. July 27, 1829, d. January, 1862, um.
92 Laura M., b. July 25, 1831, d. April 9, 1886, m. Charles O. Kellog. X

(51)

CLARK BAKER was born March 3, 1796, at Hoosick, N. Y., where he married December, 1826, Lucina Welch of Albany, N. Y. They settled first at Hoosick, but removed to Manhattan, Ill., about 1846, and he died Jan. 28, 1893. He left a very large estate, consisting of 1800 acres of land, worth $90 per acre.

Children:

93 Mary Esther, b. December, 1827.
94 Helen Maria, b. Jan. 1, 1837.
95 Clark, who died at Albany.
96 George.
97 John C.

(52)

JONATHAN BAKER was born Nov. 6, 1797, at Hoosick, N. Y., and married there March, 1818, Sarah Chapman. They first settled at Hoosick, and afterwards removed to Pompey, N. Y., where he died Feb. 12, 1830.

Children:

98 Sidney, living in Virginia, 1856.
99 Esther, living in Pittstown, N. Y., in 1856.
100 Mary, living in Syracuse, N. Y., in 1856.

(53)

NORMAN BAKER was born Oct. 27, 1799, at Hoosick, N. Y., married there January, 1827, Waity Gibbs, of Pittstown, N. Y. Died about 1863.

Children:

101 Sarah, b. October, 1833, at Pittstown, m. there September, 1855, James Carr of Pittstown.

(57)

INCREASE BAKER was born July 21, 1807, at Hoosick, N. Y., and married March 6, 1834, Julia A. Canfield of Manchester, Ontario County, New York. He died June, 1875, in Philadelphia, and was buried at Cincinnati, O.

Children:

102 Clark Arunah, b. April, 1835, at Hopewell, N. Y., d. in 1870, Cincinnati, O.
103 William Eugene, b. 1838, at Canandaigua, N. Y. X
104 Frances, b. 1840, m. Rev. Charles Amos, of Boston.
105 Albert, b. 1842, at Canandaigua, lived in Cincinnati.
106 John, b. 1850 at Cincinnati, d. there in 1872.

(58)

JIRAH BAKER was born June, 1810, at Hoosick, N. Y., married 1829, Elmira Gifford of Pittstown, N. Y., and settled at Hoosick. In 1856 they were living at Manchester, Ill.

Children: Born at Hoosick.

107 Sarah Helen.
108 Julia Esther.
109 Norman.
110 Mary Sibyl.
111 Elizabeth.
112 Clark.
113 Gideon.

(62)

BENJAMIN BAKER was born March 26, 1796, and married February, 1821, Abigal Kruyer Taylor. She was born March 28, 1801. She was the daughter of Thomas and Mary Rozena (Shouldelers) Taylor.

Children:

114 William, b. Feb. 13, 1823, d. young.
115 Mary Rozena, b. March 12, 1824, m. Dec. 16, 1847, Nathan Tanner, Sr. No children.
116 Susan Eliza, b. Dec. 20, 1830, d. May 7, 1848. Left daughter 5 weeks old (Eliza Jane).
117 Edward Orlando, b. May 5, 1834, d. Oct. 27, 1842.
118 Zerrilda Jane, b. Nov. 3, 1839, m. April 5, 1857, Emery Barrus.

Note—Nathan Tanner, Sr., died at Grantsville, Utah, Dec. 17, 1910, aged 95 years. He was considered to be the oldest member of the Mormon Church, having joined the church in 1831.

CHARLOTTE (LEAVITT) BAKER 77

ELIZABETH (STAPLES) BAKER 77   ANN (STAPLES) BAKER 77

(77)

SIMON BAKER, son of the fifth Benjamin Baker in descent, was born Oct. 18, 1811, at West Winfield, Herkemer County, New York. He died Oct. 22, 1863, at 7 p. m. of bilious fever, at Mendon, Utah, where he was buried for a short time, and was removed to Salt Lake City, and buried there in the Salt Lake City Cemetery Jan. 8, 1864, on Plat E, Block 3, Lot 5, on the south half of said lot, which title is now in the name of Jarvis Baker. The other half of the lot is in the name of Wm. Price.

Mr. Baker married first Dec. 21, 1829, at Winfield, N. Y., Mercy, daughter of Abiathar and Lydia (French) Young. She was born Jan. 27, 1807, at Poster, Providence County, R. I., and died March 4, 1845, near Montrose, Iowa.

He married second April 8, 1845, on the Mississippi River, between Nauvoo, Ill., and Montrose, Iowa, by William Snow, a Mormon Elder, Charlotte, daughter of Wiear and Abigall (Cole) Leavitt. She was born Dec. 5, 1818, in Lower Canada (see Leavitt lineage, this vol.), and died Nov. 19, 1906, at Mendon, Utah.

He married third March 18, 1853, at Salt Lake City, Utah, Elizabeth, daughter of James and Sarah (Limerick) Staples (see Staples lineage). She was born Jan. 8, 1838, at Cheltenham, Cloustershire, Eng., and died June 26, 1884, at Ogden, Utah.

He married fourth Feb. 10, 1857, at Salt Lake City, Utah, Ann, daughter of James and Sarah (Limerick) Staples. She was born April 3, 1832, at Cheltenham, England, and now (1910) resides with her son, Henry Baker, at Mesa, Arizona.

Mr. Baker resided with his parents until about 17 years of age, when he secured a position to work by the month, his father drawing his wages.

He had but $1.00 at the time of his first marriage, and that he gave to the priest. He was employed at various positions for about four years, when they removed to Pomfret, Chautauqua County, New York, where he worked at gardening for a firm by the name of Wrigleys & Co. for several years at $10.00 per month.

In the spring of 1839 the family, through the teachings of Benjamin Brown, joined the Latter-day Saints Church and removed west as far as what was then called Half Breeds Land, Lee County, Iowa. Here he located a small farm and sold it the following year and then located another, a larger farm, consisting of 80 acres of tillable land and 80 acres of timber land, built a cabin and moved into his new home in the spring of 1841. At the time he came to Iowa their possessions were small, having but one poor team of horses and an old wagon—no provisions—and but scant clothing. He was sick much of the time, and destitute, living chiefly on boiled corn, but through hard labor and perseverance, he cleared up his farm and in time collected together some stock and necessaries of life.

At this place, four of their children were born, the two youngest, twins, one of whom died two and one-half months later, and the mother who seemed unable to recover from her grief and sorrow, was taken sick and died March 4, 1845, leaving eight small children, the eldest less than 15 years old, destitute and unable to care for themselves.

On April 5, 1845, Mr. Baker found it necessary that he should get some one to care for his children, as while preparing to cross over the Mississippi River to attend conference at Nauvoo, promised his children that he would bring them home a new mother. On his way over, he asked a friend with whom he was riding, if he could refer him to some one who would make a good mother to his children, and he said, "Yes, Charlotte Leavitt, the daughter of a widow living at Nauvoo, would be a good wife and mother to your children." This occurred on April 5, 1845. So when the forenoon services were over, Mr. Baker repaired to the house of the widow, introduced himself, was invited in, and made their cottage his home during conference. While there he made his business known, and his circumstances, and Charlotte consented to go home with him and care for his children for a while, and if she liked him she would marry him; if not, he was to pay her for her services. With this understanding, on April 8, 1845, they started for home, and while crossing the Mississippi River, they concluded to marry at once, so securing the services of Elder William Snow, the ceremony was performed between the two states, thus saving a trip to the county seat for a license, as the state had no jurisdiction over marriages on the water.

The children at home, having been promised a new mother, expected him home about the 10th, and were on the lookout for them—some on top of the house, some on the wood pile, some on the fence and some in the door, all anxiously awaiting their home coming. Suddenly, as they appeared in sight, as they came around a bluff, the children all shouted simultaneously, "There she comes!" was heard from the top of the house, from the top of the fence and the wood pile, and all made a general rush for her, shouting "Mother, Mother!"

During this year, 1845, Mr. Baker put in 40 acres of corn, and raised 4,000 bushels. He shelled about 2,000 bushels and hauled it to "Mixes" and sold it at 16 cents per bushel. In the following spring of 1846 the Mormon colony was called to go to the Rocky Mountains, and Mr. Baker got together an outfit for the trip, consisting of four yoke of oxen and two wagons, one span of young horses and a light wagon, together with three or four cows and some sheep. He sold his entire farm and improvements for $300, which was consumed in purchasing the outfit as above, and leaving them with but little clothing and provisions for their journey. The family at this time consisted of Mr. Baker and wife and nine children.

After leaving this place, they went first to Mt. Pisgah, where they located for about three months. During this time Mr. Baker went down to Missouri to trade his horse team for oxen, which were considered better than horses for a journey. On his return from Missouri, he moved across the Missouri River to Winter Quarters (now Florence, Neb.), where he built a cabin for his family. He then, with some of his older boys and his teams, went down into Missouri to work, to prepare for his trip west, intending to cross to the Rocky Mountains with the first company of Mormons. During the winter he procured a scanty outfit for such an undertaking, but before starting, he counselled with his family, and put the matter to a vote, whether they should undertake such a perilous journey with such a large family, and in their destitute condition—suffice it to say that the family vote was unanimous to start on their journey.

His outfit now for the journey consisted of four wagons and ox teams, taking with them Mrs. Phoebe Leavitt (his wife's step-mother) and his large family of children, the total number of persons 15, including Mrs. Leavitt and her children, Emiline, George and Louisa Leavitt; the children having neither hats nor shoes and were very destitute of other clothing.

Leaving Florence about May 1, 1847, they went out to Elk Horn River, where the Saints met in camp to organize in companies to cross the plains. Their company was the third 100 of the emigrating Saints. Their organization consisted of Amos Neff, captain of 10; Joseph B. Noble, captain of 50, and Jedediah M. Grant, captain of 100, who was over the other captains. When their organization was completed, the company started on their march through the wilderness to the Rocky Mountains. As they journeyed on, they found that their teams were too heavily loaded, so they yoked up their cows, their steers and any and everything that could work. The country was inhabited by many Indians, who never saw a white man before, and when they reached the North Platte country, there were hundreds of thousands of buffaloes. Their teams would frequently become frightened and stampede on sight of these large herds of buffaloes. Mr. Baker had an old shotgun, sawed off at both ends, which he called a "Pistoloon," with which he killed many buffaloes while crossing the plains, thus supplying the camp and his family with meat. They were at Sweet Water Sept. 9, and on Oct. 2, 1847, they arrived in what is now Salt Lake City, where Mr. Baker pitched his tent and began making preparations for the winter, building a cabin and procuring fire wood for their use. On arriving in Salt Lake Valley, remote from civiizaltion in a strange land in the midst of a savage warlike tribe of Indians, their little band of 1,500 souls had to use caution and diplomacy for protection. They treated the Indians kindly, and gained their good will, and as a further precaution, they built three forts for protection. The "Old Fort" being built of adobes, the North Fort and the South Fort were built of logs. The Indians, seeing that they were prepared to defend themselves, committed no depredations, except to occasionally kill some of the white men's stock.

Their rations while crossing the plains and during the first winter were but one-half pound of flour per day for each person, this with poor beef, rawhide, and thistle roots, which served as vegetables, was their food for the winter of 1848. The thistles that year grew spontaneously and it is said they have never grown since. About May 1 the roots of the thistle became tough; they then used the tops for greens, until their crop of grain was ripe, which they threshed out and ground in a hand mill, making their bread of this chopped wheat.

This year, 1848, Mr. Baker made the first molasses in Utah. It was made from cornstalks and the mill was made with wooden rollers, the squeaking of which could be heard a long distance off while in motion.

During the year of 1849, hundreds of gold seekers on their way to California, came through Salt Lake City. Their stock being poor, they were forced to sell them and buy fat teams with which to continue their journey, selling groceries cheap, and paying high prices for flour. This exchange made times good for the Utah people.

At this time, 1849 and 1850, Mr. Baker procured some Indian ponies and provisions and exchanged commodities and outfits, etc., with the gold seekers, exchanging fat ponies for jaded horses, which his boys would take care of on good feed, and soon have them in order to exchange for others, thus making several trades and exchanges during the season of 1850, and the results were that at the end of the season Mr. Baker had accumulated 25 yoke of oxen, 12 cows, 6 horses, 3 new wagons, blankets, clothing, and camp equipage by the wagon load, together with considerable money. That fall, they moved from south of Salt Lake City to the mouth of River Jordan on the west side and took up winter quarters.

In 1849 he served as militia man in the Indian War at Battle Creek (now Pleasant Grove), Utah Valley (now Utah county), about five weeks.

During the fall of 1850, Mr. Baker was called to go south of Salt Lake about 250 miles and locate a colony there, so getting together an outfit, he, together with his son, Joseph, and his son-in-law, John Topham, who had married his daughter, Betsie, and about 200 others, started late in December for their new location, and located in what is now Parawan, in Iron county, Utah. The following spring, being released from this mission, he turned over his location to his son-in-law, John Topham, and returned to Salt Lake City, when he was given another mission, which was to go and work with his whole force (of boys and teams) in a canyon, called "Baker's Canyon," eight miles north of Salt Lake City. There they commenced work for the church in April, 1851, and continued in this work each season until 1855 or 1856.

On July 25, 1855, Bryant Stringham, as captain, with Simon Baker and Andrew Moffet as his councilmen, together with Joseph Baker, Brigham Young, Jr., Thomas Clayton, Thomas Naylor, Thomas Kendall and George Twist, explored Cache Valley, and located the Church Farm as a place where the Church could range their cattle, so he was pioneer, not only of Salt Lake City, but also of Iron County, Cache County and later of Carson Valley, Nevada. By this time,

1855, Mr. Baker had prospered, and with the assistance of his boys, had accumulated about 350 head of cattle, and went over into Cache Valley to look up a range for them.

THE CARSON MISSION.

During the spring of 1856 Mr. Baker was called to go and assist in the colonization of Carson Valley. He had just completed a house on his lot at the corner of First North and West Temple street(this lot is now: Lot 1, Block 104, Plat A., S. L. City Survey), and before starting on this mission, one of the Apostles of the Latter-day Saint Church came to him and said: "Brother Baker, before going on this mission, we want you to do something for us to help pay off the church debt." Mr. Baker replied: "Whatever is required of me, I am ready to do." The reply was: "We want fifty head of your best cattle, and also want you to turn over to the Perpetual Emigration Fund, your house and lot."

Mr. Baker turned the property over to the church, as requested, and with his wife, Elizabeth, and sons, Albert and Joseph, started on this mission. There were about two hundred people called to go at this time and settle in Carson Valley, with instructions to buy out the settlers who had preceded them. Carson Valley at this time belonged to Utah and was termed Carson County.

Genoa, the oldest town in Nevada, being the first white settlement on the east side of the Sierra Nevada Mountains, was settled by emigrants a few years previous to the advent of this Colony, at which time there were about thirty families in that vicinity. Carson County was settled in 1851 by Col. John Reese.

Mr. Baker bought the Niles and Sears farm, situated about four miles north of Genoa and about eight miles south of Carson City, between the two towns, paying $2,500 worth of cattle and horses for it.

This Mission was presided over by Orson Hyde. They were under the Utah organization of government with Orson Hyde as Probate Judge, who then held Criminal and Appellate jurisdiction. The Church organization was presided over by William Nixon as president of the Genoa branch and Richard Bently as president of the Warsaw branch, north of Carson City. There were neither wards nor Bishops there at that time.

Among those who were there of this colony may be mentioned: Orson Hyde, Simon Baker, Joseph Baker, Albert M. Baker, William Nixon, Captain Alfred Higgins, Peregreen Sessions, Richard Bently, William Price, John D. Chase, Charles Harper, Geo. Billings, Abraham Hunsaker, James Murdock, Isaac Hunter, Abraham Coon, John Walker, William Kay, Enoch Coney, Geo. Beckstead, Christopher Layton, William Jennings, James Clawson, Samuel Moore and Christopher Merkley.

On their arrival at Carson Valley, about July 1, Mr. Baker, after buying his farm and making some improvements, with his son Albert, went over into California for supplies, and after their return and making some preparations for winter, Elder Orson Hyde, their mission president, called on Mr. Baker to return with him to Salt Lake City. So, leaving Genoa about December 1, 1856, they started on the perilous trip of 700 miles, which nearly cost them their lives through exposure, cold and hunger. Arriving at his home on the Jordan River, five weeks later, he found all well with an abundance of provisions.

The following spring Mr. Baker returned to Carson Valley, arriving there about June 1, and on June 12, he and his son, Joseph, started over the Sierra Nevada Mountains for California to find his son, Jarvis, who went there in 1850. They found him, sick, on Secret Ravine, in Placer County, where he had located a mining claim, which he sold with the encumbrance to his partner for $10, and returned with his father to Genoa, where he soon recovered his health.

Soon after his return from California, on account of the impending trouble with Johnston's Army, the mission was abandoned. So, selling his possessions for $1,200, he returned to Salt Lake City, arriving there the early part of August, 1857.

Note—Friday, Aug. 14, 1857, a company of Carson Valley settlers returned to Great Salt Lake City.

October, 1857, the "Mormon" settlements in Carson Valley were broken up. Most of the settlers returned to Salt Lake City early in November.

William Reed Smith of Centerville was made captain of the Carson Colony, which left Carson Valley near the middle of September and arrived in Salt Lake City during the following month. Church Chronology.

THE MOVE SOUTH.

When the call was made to move south, Mr. Baker started two or three of his teams moving the poor families who had no teams, as far south as the Provo bottoms, where many families located and lived in cane wigwams during the summer. He then moved his own family, starting south about May 10, 1858, locating on the shores of Utah Lake, where they remained until August, it being a good place to care for their stock, and procure an abundance of fish for the family.

The following from Bancroft's History of Utah gives a better history of the times and events than the writer is able to portray:

"The rays of the rising sun slant athwart the bayonets of the Fifth Infantry as forming the van of the Union Army, it approaches the outskirts of Salt Lake, at dusk is still heard in its streets the rumble of caisons and baggage wagons. But no other sound is heard, save the murmur of the creek, nor is there sign of life in the city of the Saints. Zion is deserted!

Thirty thousand of the Mormons had left their homes in Salt Lake City and the northern settlements, taking with them all their movable effects and leaving only in the former, a score of men, with instructions to apply the torch, if it should be occupied by the troops.

The outer doors were locked, and in the vacant dwellings were heaps of straw, shavings and wood ready for the work of destruction.

In April when, Governor Cummings first arrived in the city, he reported that the people were already moving from the northern settlements. The roads were filled with wagons laden with provisions and household furniture; by their side women and children, many of them so thinly clad that their garments barely covered their nakedness, some being attired only in sacking, some with no covering but a remnant of a rag carpet, and some barefooted and bleeding, tramped through the deep snow, journeying they knew not whither, no more than at the exodus of Nauvoo; but it was "the will of the Lord" or rather of their prophet.

Returning with the peace commissioners, the governor repaired to the house of Elder Staines, and found the place abandoned. Tullidge relates that at the Elder's house a cold lunch was spread for the governor, and in the garden loads of straw were significantly heaped up.

Inquiring the cause of the silence that pervaded the city, Mrs. Cummings was told that the Mormons had resolved to burn it, if the Army should attempt its occupation. "How terrible," she exclaimed, "it has the appearance of a city that has been afflicted with a plague, every house looks like a tomb of the dead; for two miles I have seen but one man in it. Poor creatures, so all have left their hard earned homes." Bursting into tears, she turned to her husband, "Oh, Alfred," she said, "something must be done to bring them back; don't permit the army to stay in the city. Can't you do something for them?" "Yes, Madam," he replied, "I shall do all I can, rest assured."

A few days after the conference with the commissioners, Cummings followed the Mormons 50 miles to the southward, pleaded with them, at first in vain, but finally induced them to return.

The army moved out to Cedar Valley, about 40 miles southwest of Salt Lake City, where they established Camp Floyd.

After returning from the south, Mr. Baker devoted most of his time to farming and stock raising. In addition to his Jordan farm, he built a house on the lot adjoining the one he had given to the church, as stated in the foregoing, and moved into it.

About September 25, 1863, Mr. Baker and his wife Elizabeth and family moved to Mendon, Utah, taking them about 75 head of stock, intending to locate a home there, but Mr. Baker became sick on his way, and on their arrival in Mendon they moved into the house of his son, G. W. Baker, where he remained bedfast, and being dangerously ill, a team was sent to Salt Lake City for his wife Charlotte, that she might see him while yet alive.

Of his family there were present at the Semi-Centennial Jubilee held in Salt Lake City, Utah, July 24, 1897, his wife, Charlotte and children, Amenzo W., Albert M., Betsie, George W., Joseph, Rebecca, Sarah, Abigail, Wiear, Samuel, Hannah and Maria.

AUTOBIOGRAPHY OF SIMON BAKER, WRITTEN ABOUT 1846.

"I, Simon Baker, was born Oct. 18, 1811, in the town of Winfield, Herkimer County, state of New York. My father and mother, Benjamin and Rebecca, were born in the state of Massachusetts.

"I lived in the town where I was born till I was 18 years old. I then married Mercy Young, daughter of Abiathar and Lydia Young, Dec. 31, 1829.

"I moved to Chautauqua County, New York, in 1833. I embraced the Gospel 1839. I then, through the mercy and goodness of God, had power to get means, together with the Saints. I and my wife were baptized into the Church by Benjamin Brown. I have since lived with the Saints. I was ordained into the Seventies Quorum at the October Conference, 1844. There were born to my wife Mercy five sons and four daughters. My daughter, Mary, died when eleven weeks old, 1843, and my wife Mercy died March 4, 1845.

"I married my wife, Charlotte, April 8, 1845. I feel thankful that I am permitted to live in this age of the world. My desire is that I may keep the commandments of God and be saved in His Celestial Kingdom."

Children: First wife, Mercy Young.

119 Jarvis Young, b. Nov. 13, 1830, West Winfield, N. Y. X
120 Amenzo White, b. Jan. 19, 1832, West Winfield, N. Y. X
121 Albert Mowry, b. Oct. 3, 1833, Pomfret, Chautauqua County, New York. X.
122 Betsie, b. Jan. 24, 1835, Pomfret, m. John Topham. X
123 Geo. Washington, b. Sept. 9, 1837, Pomfret, N. Y. X
124 Joseph, b. Aug. 15, 1839, Lee County, Iowa. X
125 Rebecca, b. June 9, 1841, Lee County, Iowa, m. first William Price, second Snellon Marion Johnson. X
126 Mary, b. July 3, 1843, Lee County, Iowa, d. there Sept. 18, 1843.
127 Sarah, b. July 3, 1843, Lee County, Iowa, m. Wm. C. Farnsworth. X

Children: Second wife, Charlotte Leavitt.

128 Abigail, b. Jan. 7, 1846, Nauvoo, Ill., m. Thos. Mathews. X

129 Benjamin, b. July 6, 1847, Dogtown, Neb., m. Margaret A. Rowe. X
130 Charlotte, b. April 5, 1849, Salt Lake City, m. William Longstroth. X
131 Simon, b. Nov. 20, 1850, Salt Lake City, d. there April 4, 1851.
132 Phoebe, b. Aug. 27, 1852, Bountiful, Utah, d. Mendon, Utah.
133 Wiear, b. July 20, 1854, Salt Lake City. X
134 Samuel L., b. June 26, 1856, Salt Lake City. X
135 Hannah, b. Dec. 28, 1857, Salt Lake City, m. Wm. Willie. X
136 Jeremiah, b. June 18, 1860, Salt Lake City, m. Mary T. Lemon. X

Children: Third wife, Elizabeth Staples.

137 Sarah Ann, b. Aug. 19, 1854, Salt Lake City, Utah, d. there March 8, 1856.
138 James Staples, b. Aug. 25, 1856, Genoa, Nev. X
139 Elizabeth, b. July 8, 1858, Salt Lake City, Utah, m. Spencer D. Shumway. X
140 Maria, b. Nov. 8, 1860, Salt Lake City, Utah, m. Merlin J. Stone. X
141 Mercy, b. July 15, 1863, Salt Lake City, Utah, d. February, 1865, Corn Creek, Utah.

Children: Fourth wife, Ann Staples.

142 Henry, b. Jan. 2, 1858, Salt Lake City, Utah. X

(86)

ROSWELL P. BAKER was born November 7, 1818, in Spafford, N. Y. Married Elizabeth ——. He died Dec. 22, 1869.
Children:
143 A child, d. at birth.
144 Alida, b. Dec. 22, 1856, m. November, 1896, Charles Hoephi. X
145 Jennie, b. October, 1861.
146 Nellie, b. April 9, 1864, m. Azariah Hulet. No children.

(87)

ASHBEL S. BAKER was born Nov. 3, 1820, in Spafford, N. Y. Died Dec. 25, 1849. Married Sarah A. ——. Second, Novissa ——.
Children: First wife.
147 Sarah A., b. April 25, 1845, m. Randolph B. Rollo. No children.
Children: Second wife.
148 Charles, b. July 18, 1847, d. July 10, 1864.
149 Clarissa E., b. Oct. 21, 1849, m. William Boyle. X

(89)

MARQUIS D. BAKER was born December 27, 1824, at Spafford, N. Y., and died Dec. 6, 1890. He married Caroline ——.
Children:
150 Mark, b. Feb. 23, 1861, d. September, 1861.
151 Carrie, b. Dec. 20, 1868, d. March 22, 1870.
152 Eugene, b. Sept. 5, 1871.

(103)

WILLIAM E. BAKER was born 1838 at Cayuga County, New York. Married in 1864 in Illinois, Sarah Chesebro. Residence, Pontiac, Ill. Treasurer of Livingston County 1893. Came to Livingston County, Illinois, in 1859, where he has since resided, except two years in Utah, Idaho and Montana, in 1864 and 1865.
Children:
153 Albert I., b. Dec. 1, 1865.
154 Clark E., b. April 7, 1867.
155 Helen M., b. 1869.
156 Gertrude, b. 1871, d. June, 1874.
157 Della M., b. 1875.
158 Stevens, b. 1878.
159 Isabel, b. 1880

JARVIS YOUNG BAKER 119   RACHEL (RICHARDS) BAKER 119

JARVIS YOUNG BAKER, eldest son of Simon and Mercy Young Baker, was born Nov. 13, 1830, at West Winfield, Herkermer County, New York. He married Rachel Richards, daughter of John and Agnes Hill Richards, Dec. 25, 1864, at Mendon, Cache County, Utah.

He was a strong vigorous man, five feet and ten inches in height, and his weight varying from 165 to 175 pounds. He was light complexioned and quick in thought and act.

He was faithful in his work. Honest to the letter; who considered his word as good as his bond. He was courageous, independent and persevering, always accomplishing whatever he decided to do. Characteristics which were prominent in his childhood, endowments which nature seemed to have given him at birth.

A cousin, Samuel Stillman, who knew him when he was a baby, made the following statement in a letter to his brother Amenzo: "You say your brother, Jarvis, died May, 1891. He was the only one of your father's children, except yourself, that I ever saw. I distinctly remember the first day he walked alone. Your father and mother were living in one part of my father's home and that morning Jarvis learned to go alone. I saw him creep to a chair by the window and get upon his feet. He then turned around facing an open door, and at once and of his own volition ran across the room as fast as he could toward the open door, when he fell flat on the floor. He did not cry, but crept back to the chair, got up, tried it over again with the same result, but after several attempts he was able to go all around the room without help. That was a long time ago, but I remember the courage and perseverance of that little child as well as if it had been but yesterday."

When a boy, though small of his age, he was strong and healthy, and was put to work when very young. His father's family being in humble circumstances and he being the eldest child, responsibility was placed on him very early in life; the result of which had made him, by the time he was fourteen years of age, more competent, efficient and trustworthy in his labor than boys many years his senior.

When he was three years of age his parents moved to Pomfret, Chautauqua County, New York, where his father took charge of a sawmill. The family lived near the mill. One day when he was out playing he ventured out on the logs which were floating in the millpond. When near the center he lost his balance and fell into the water. His mother came to the door of the home just in time to see her little son disappear beneath the logs. There being no one near to render assistance, she went to the pond, ran over the logs, drew the boy from the water and carried him back safely to the shore over the treacherous turning logs.

In 1839 he moved with his parents to Montrose, Lee County, Iowa. At this place in 1840, he was baptized and confirmed a member of the Church of Jesus Christ of Latter-day Saints by David Pettigrew.

A new farm was taken up and he assisted his father with the work. Here March 4, 1845, he was called upon to meet one of the greatest trials of his life, the loss of his beloved mother, whose memory he ever held sacred and of whom he always spoke with the greatest love and reverence.

After leaving Pomfret his advantages for education were limited. Schools were few and far between, and the family being in such humble circumstances his assistance to his father was so urgent that if schools had been accessible attendance would have been impossible. However, through his persistent efforts, he succeeded in acquiring a comparatively good education. He formed the habit of reading and studied arithmetic by himself. He took advantage of schools when the opportunity presented itself. After he had grown to be a man, he attended school in California. He became a good penman and quite proficient in geography and history. He was also acquainted with the works of the authors and topics of the times in which he lived.

When the Latter-day Saints were expelled from Nauvoo, the

family moved with them, first to Mt. Pisgah, Iowa, and about three months later, in August, 1846, to Winter Quarters, where they spent that notable winter of 1846-7.

Here Jarvis was of no little value in the great movement. When the people were confronted in their advance by the Missouri River, there were no bridges on which to cross, and it would have taken some time for the wagons and oxen to pass over on the small ferryboat. If the cattle could be forced to swim across the river it would expediate the task. There was no one, however, who cared to risk himself in undertaking this perilous trip. After some deliberation, Simon Baker overcame the difficulty by placing his son, Jarvis, upon one of his trusty oxen, which was yoked to another and started him in the lead of the herd; which entered the river in great confusion. Much joy was expressed and praise given when the boy at the head of the herd emerged safely on the opposite shore.

During the winter he made two trips with his father to Missouri to get supplies to take on their journey west.

In the spring of 1847, when the people commenced their westward march to the Rocky Mountain, times were hard, money scarce, and he and his younger brothers had very little food to eat, on account of its scarcity. They were allowed a small portion of food each day, which they called rations, and with no shoes to protect their feet from the parching sand, no hats to shield them from the relentless rays of the sun, they plodded on their journey by the side of their ox teams, and at night took their turn standing guard to help protect the company from the wild animals and savage Indians which often beset their way.

They arrived in Salt Lake Valley, Oct. 2, 1847, in the company presided over by Jedediah M. Grant. At once he and his father began work in the canyon getting out timber for a new home, which they had completed before spring. All the lumber and logs used in the construction of the home were cut with a whip-saw. At one end of which, standing in a pit he worked day after day, early and late, oftentimes so weak through exposure and lack of proper food that he could scarcely pull the saw.

When spring opened they began tilling the soil, planting the seed they had brought with them. The first year's crop was poor. Few vegetables were raised. Therefore, many of the wild plants were gathered and used for food. The plant of greatest value was the thistle root which finally became one of the most important vegetables. With this vegetable he and his brother, Amenzo, provided the family. The corn crop failed to mature and in order to prevent a total loss of the crop, he was put in charge of a molasses mill, which his father had invented. The ears and leaves were stripped from the stalks of corn. The juice was extracted from the stalks by means of the wooden rollers of the mill. This juice was boiled into molasses, and thus the people of Salt Lake saved their crop, which otherwise would have been a failure.

He went to California in 1850 and engaged in mining. While there he was stricken with mountain fever which came near proving fatal. In 1857 he returned to Salt Lake City.

During the fall of 1859, he, with others, was called by President Brigham Young to enlist in the Mormon Army, under General Burton to go as guards to intercept Johnston's Army, which was at that time approaching Utah. His labors on this mission were earnestly and faithfully discharged.

In 1864, having been put in administrator of his father's estate, he went to Mendon, Cache County, Utah, to look after the property located there; his father having died at this place October, 1863.

He finally made Mendon his home. Soon after his arrival there he became acquainted with Rachel Richards, whom he married December 25, 1864.

A short time after he arrived at Mendon there was an uprising of the Indians in the northern part of Utah and the southern part of Idaho. He, with other members of the Utah militia, went to that place to help quell the trouble. His company was fortunate, the trouble being settled before they reached the place.

He held the office of an Elder in the church and was an ardent worker in church undertakings. When the people of Mendon adopted the law of consecration or United Order, he was an earnest worker for the cause.

In 1876 he made his permanent home on his farm near Mendon, where he died May 27, 1891, after a brief illness of one week, leaving his wife and eleven living children, one child having died several years before.

MRS. RACHEL RICHARDS BAKER, daughter of John and Agnes Hill Richards, was born July 27, 1846, in a covered wagon on the bank of the Mississippi River, near Montrose, in Lee County, Iowa. Her parents, with many others, had just been expelled from Nauvoo by a mob. The hostility and the threats of which compelled the company to move up the river when she was three days old. Through the exposure and the hardships the mother and the child had been compelled to endure, she was taken very sick. Many times while she was ill the parents thought the little life had gone out, but through faith and the tender care of Mrs. Angel, a kind and skillful nurse, she was restored to her wanted health.

Her father bought a farm on the Honey Creek, located a few miles from Kanesville, in Pottawattamie County, Iowa, and commenced farming, thinking he could in this way provide himself with food and the necessary means to take himself and family West. At this place when she was about four years of age, while crossing the Honey Creek on a log footbridge, she fell into the water and would have drowned if her brother, John, had not been near and caught her by the hair in time to save her. It was often said that it was by her beautiful head of hair, combined with the assistance of her courageous brother, that her life was saved. Again she came near losing her life in 1851 when the family were on their way to Utah. She fell from the front end of their wagon; the wheel of this heavily-loaded vehicle passed over her right shoulder and head, leaving her unconscious and apparently dead. Her brother, John' again came to her assistance. He pulled her from under the-wagon just in time to prevent the back wheel from running over her. Her mother took her in her arms and administered to her and soon she recovered from the accident. It seems that providence was ever at hand to provide assistance in times of danger.

On the arrival of her parents in Utah, they located at Mill Creek. Here she entered school; later she attended school in Salt Lake City. Her first school books, consisting of a speller and a reader, were bought with the money she received for wheat that she had gleaned in the harvest field.

In 1857, when Salt Lake Valley was vacated on account of Johnston's Army, she went with her father's family to Santaquin, Utah County, returning to Salt Lake City the following year, and in 1859 moved to Mendon, Cache County, Utah, arriving there Christmas day.

She grew up a beautiful, kind and unselfish girl, just and honest, sacrificing her own pleasures for the comforts of others. Her beautiful character won her many worthy and lasting friends. At Mendon she became acquainted with Jarvis Young Baker, and was married to him at this place December 25, 1864. From this marriage she became the mother of twelve children, six boys and six girls, all of whom grew to manhood and womanhood except one little girl, Elizabeth, who died when small. Her husband died when most of her children were young, her baby, Chester, being about two years old. She was left with little means with which to support her family. She passed through many trials and hardships in rearing it. Reverse circumstances often crossing her path. But ever courageous and economical, never complaining, she struggled on. Keeping her family together until her children had almost reached maturity, when her three youngest sons were taken from her by the hand of death. Her son, Hyrum, being killed in a railroad wreck. A few months later Asa was frozen to death while out hunting, and the year following Chester died of pneumonia. This terrible blow was borne with patience, long suffering and without complaint. She is at the present time living at her home in Mendon, Utah.

Children: Born at Mendon.
160 Mercy Rachel, b. Sept. 29, 1865. X
161 Jarvis Alexander, b. April 18, 1867, m. Pauline Pefferle. X
162 Mary Agnes, b. Aug. 29, 1870, m. Carl Andrew Nyman. X
163 Elizabeth Orilla, b. July 5, 1873, d. May 11, 1878, Mendon, Utah. X
164 Lucy Maria, b. June 21, 1875. X
165 John Daniel, b. March 26, 1877. X

166 Lydia Aurelia, b. April 6, 1879, m. James Christian Hogeson. X
167 Emma Theresa, b. Sept. 7, 1880, m. Fred Jacob Sorenson. X
168 Simon Moroni, b. April 16, 1882. X
169 Hyrum LeRoy, b. March 27, 1885, d. Feb. 2, 1905, Milton, North Dakota. X
170 Asa Norman, b. Nov. 25, 1886, d. Dec. 4, 1905, Mendon, Utah. X
171 Noah Chester, b. March 13, 1889, d. Jan. 18, 1907, Park City, Utah. X

AMENZO W. BAKER, SR. 120

AGNES (STEELE) BAKER 120

(120)
AMENZO WHITE BAKER.
By George W. Baker, Sr.

AMENZO WHITE BAKER, son of Simon and Mercy (Young) Baker, was born June 9, 1832, at West Winfield, Herkermer County, New York. Soon after his birth the family removed to Pomfret, Chautauqua County, New York, where they resided until 1839, when they became Proselytes of the Mormon faith and moved west to Iowa, which was then a territory. At this place he attended the village school and assisted in the labor on their new farm until the spring of 1846, when during the "exodus" of the Mormons from Illinois, he, together with his parents, left their new farm and joined the fleeing camps of Mormons, who continued their march to Mt. Pisgah, Iowa, where they remained until the following August, when they moved across the river and went into Winter Quarters. During the winter of 1846-7 he went with his father, some 300 miles into the state of Missouri, to work for provisions for their journey to the Rocky Mountains.

In May, 1847, the family started on their march for the west, Mr. Baker being assigned to drive two yoke of oxen on one wagon, maintained this position until they arrived in Salt Lake City, Oct. 2, 1847, where he assisted his father in getting out material for their house and making preparations for the winter. Being short of provisions and as there was an abundance of thistles in the bottoms, about one mile south of the fort, Mr. Baker was assigned the duty of gathering thistle roots with which he supplied the family during the winter of 1847-8. The following spring he assisted his father in putting in some crops and in the fall helped him gather what little they had raised, mostly corn, damaged by an early frost, necessitating an early harvest; his father being forced to economize, determined to make the best of his misfortunes, so while the boys were cutting and stripping the blades from the cornstalks, made a wooden mill to press them, and from which he made molasses. This proved to be a success and with Mr. Baker as one of the chief operators, he continued in this business until the fall of 1849, attending occasionally a winter school.

In 1851 he went with his father to work in what was afterwards called Baker's Canyon, in Davis County, where he labored until the fall of 1853, when he, together with his brother, George W. and some fifty others, were called on a mission to the Indians, where they built Fort Supply, at what is now Robertson, Wyo., and labored at farming and preaching to the Indians, until the fall of 1856. This year Mr. Baker raised a good crop, and this being one of those experimental years in hand-cart emigration, several of the rear companies were caught in the deep early snow in a destitute condition; this being reported to President Young, a call was made for volunteers with good teams and wagons, to go to their rescue and bring them in to Salt Lake City. Mr. Baker volunteered for the trip, and being 100 miles to the east of Salt Lake City, it gave him and his Fort Supply comrades 100 miles the lead of the Salt Lake City volunteers, so traveling east until they met the rear companies, bringing them on until they overtook the next company, etc. Here Mr. Baker experienced the most heart-rending scenes of his life; women and children, almost naked, in snow to their knees, some with frozen feet, and almost famished with cold and hunger. Here he performed the heroic acts of his life, in helping and caring for those unfortunate beings; he seems to have had the courage of a lion to have accomplished what he did. Some one or more of those unfortunate died each night, so there was a burial every morning, before breaking camp.

On one occasion they buried 16 persons in one grave or pit. He continued his labors with those people until they arrived at Fort Bridger, when he was relieved by fresh recruits from Salt Lake City, and returned to his home at Fort Supply, some 12 miles to the south.

During the early summer of this year, 1856, Mr. Baker and his companion, Mr. James Brown, were out among the Indians, preaching and traveling from one camp to another, when, in a lonely place, they were surprised by a renegade band of Navajo Indians, who, while they were hostile towards the United States soldiers, were friendly with the Mormons. These Indians were out of their own territory and in the territory of the Snake Indians, to whom Mr. Baker and Mr. Brown were preaching.

Mr. Baker wearing a United States soldier coat, the Navajos thought they were "Americans," a name they applied to all United States soldiers, so surrounded the missionaries, who, though they did not understand the Navajo language, put up a vigorous protest in the Snake Indian tongue, and as there was one among the Navajos who could speak a little of the Snake Indian language, after making examination of their underwear, found they were Mormons, and through his explanations to the others, they were released. Mr. Baker had many thrilling experiences while on this mission, continuing his travels among the Snake Indians until the invasion of Johnston's Army in 1857, when the little colony at Fort Supply, abandoned their homes, which they had been four years in establishing, burned their buildings, grain and improvements, to prevent their occupation by the troops.

After being released from this command, he returned to his father's home in Salt Lake City, arriving there December 26, 1857, making this his home during the winter, and in the following spring of 1858 he took an active part in helping to move the poor families from Salt Lake City to Provo, Utah County, duirng the exodus of the "Saints" to the south.

President Young had given orders to vacate Salt Lake City, and all the northern settlements in Utah, and to leave their homes ready for the torch. After all the people had abandoned their homes and moved to the south, Mr. Baker, together with about 200 others, was detailed as a secret guard to keep in hiding, to apply the torch to every house if conditions should require it. Remaining in the city until July, when a treaty was made with the Government Commissioners, and all of the people returned to their homes.

He engaged in sundry employments the balance of the summer and the following winter attended school, having had but little opportunity for schooling in earlier life.

The spring of 1859 found Mr. Baker preparing for a trip to his native state, New York, to visit relatives and collect Genealogy, working his way to Omaha by driving a four-mule team, and returning in the fall, worked his way back to Salt Lake City, as a matter of economy. The following winter he assisted in feeding the stock on his father's ranch, on the Jordan River, and in the spring of 1860, having concluded to try and make himself another home, he, in com-

This is the "Company House" built by Amenzo W. Baker, Albert M. Baker, Sr., and Geo. W Baker in the fall of 1860 at Mendon, Cache County, Utah. Geo. W. Baker at corner of house.

pany with his brothers, Albert M. and George W., gathered together an outfit of agricultural implements and started for Cache Valley April 5, 1860, arriving in Mendon on April 18, 1860.

These Baker brothers co-operated in their labors during 1860 and 1861, building a company cabin and corrals, all living together as one family. During this time he was enrolled as one of the home guards, under military discipline, which was necessary in all the new settlements of the Valley at this time, to protect themselves against the Indians, who were much displeased with the white man's encroachments in taking their land and catching their fish, and gave the colonies much trouble. He was subject to the military for about two years, working when off duty, in the canyons and on the farm, getting material together to build a home for himself, and was successful in his efforts in procuring a comfortable home. In 1861-2 he taught the first school in Mendon, Utah.

In 1862 he was called to go to Omaha to assist in bringing the Mormon emigration to Utah; driving an eight-ox team from Mendon to Omaha, returning the same season, which required five months time for the round trip. Mr Baker made himself so efficient on this trip that he was called to make a second trip the next year, 1863, thus making him a record of having driven ox teams across the plains five times, a distance of 5,125 miles under campaign discipline, besides having driven an ox team at home, for all of his team work, for a period of forty years, would give him a record of at least 25,000 miles, as a world's record for ox team driving.

The following year, 1864, he worked on his farm and improved his new home, and in the fall having harvested a good crop, and feeling that he was able to feed and shelter more than himself, and that it was not good to be alone, he married Nov. 19, 1864, Agnes, daughter of Hamilton and Jane (Martin) Steele. She was born Dec. 25, 1833, at Galston, Ayrshire, Scotland.

Mrs. Baker at the age of 17, while in Scotland, became a member of the Latter-day Saints Church on June 15, 1851, and sailed from Liverpool for America Nov. 19, 1855, on the Sail Ship Columbia, landing at New York Jan. 1, 1856, and went direct from there to Lawrence, Mass., making her home with her brother, Alexander Steel, and working at the steam loom factory until the spring of 1859, when with her brother and his family, made the trip across the plains to Utah, arriving in Salt Lake City early in the fall.

She married first Nov. 26, 1859, John Hill. He was a widower with five children. On March 1, 1860, they moved to Wellsville, Cache County, where her husband and one of his brothers built and operated a grist-mill the following fall. Here at Wellsville the following children were born to them: Jane Morton, born Sept. 23, 1860; Archibald and Janett, twins, born Jan. 18, 1862, and Frances, born June 30, 1863. On Aug. 30, 1863, while her husband was in the brush between Wellsville and Hyrum, he was mistaken for a bear, and instantly killed by a party of hunters from Hyrum. This left her in sad circumstances, with a family of nine children to care for.

After her marriage to Mr. Baker, she went to his home in Mendon, Utah, where her husband worked on his small farm and continued to drive oxen on the farm and in the canyons until 1874, when he filed on 160 acres of railroad land adjoining Mendon City, which he afterwards bought, and in erecting better buildings, planting out a large orchard, he improved the new tract of land, until he had one of the best farms in that vicinity.

Mrs. Baker died Nov. 11, 1904, at her home in Mendon, Utah. She was a noble woman of sterling character, a true wife, mother, friend and neighbor. This was the saddest misfortune of Mr. Baker's eventful life. It seemed to break him down in health and spirits more than all else, but, having three grown daughters at home, he was enabled to continue housekeeping.

His health continued poor for three years following the death of his wife, when he was stricken with pneumonia, from which he died seven days later, on July 13, 1907, surrounded by his children and many loving friends; thus ended the career of a great man, a good Christian, kind husband, loving father, patriotic citizen and a good neighbor.

Children: All born at Mendon, Utah.
172 Amenzo White, b. Nov. 3, 1865, single.
173 Mary Elizabeth, b. June 2, 1866, d. March 11, 1868.
174 Hamilton Simon, b. July 1, 1868, m. Christina Sorenson. X
175 Agnes Mercy, b. June 6, 1870, d. March 13, 1888.
176 Sarah Margaret, b. Aug. 19, 1872, m. Joseph Johnson. X
177 Alexander Steele, b. May 17, 1874, m. Margarite Ouena Morgan.
178 Hannah Maria, b. Oct. 23, 1875, m. David Buist. X
   X.
179 Charlotte Annie, b. March 22, 1880, m. Claude L. Johnson Nov. 9, 1908. X

ALBERT MOWRY BAKER, SR. 121

JANE MARIA (CURTIS) BAKER 121 EDNA JANE (COON) BAKER 121

ALBERT MOWRY BAKER, son of Simon, was born Oct. 3, 1833, at Pomfret, Chautauqua County, New York. He was married in Salt Lake City, Utah, Dec. 25, 1854, to Jane Maria, daughter of Charles and Sarah (Wright) Curtis. She was born Nov. 14, 1833, at Holbeach, Lincolnshire, England, and emigrated with her parents to Utah in 1853.

Mr. Baker was named in honor of his cousin, Albert Mowry. (See Mowry family, this vol.)

He married second April 11, 1865, at Salt Lake City, Utah, Edna Jane, daughter of Abraham and Elizabeth (Wilson) Coon. She was born Sept. 30, 1848, in Pottawattamie County, Iowa. He died at Mendon, Cache County, Utah, Sept. 3, 1909, aged 75 years and eleven months.

Mr. Baker's parents resided at Pomfret for a number of years after his birth, where his father had charge of a saw mill, the family living in a cabin near the mill.

One day as Albert was reaching for a willow that grew near the water's edge, he fell into the swift current, which carried him down through the mill, and through an old barrel at the bottom of the mill race, and on down the stream, where he was rescued by his brothers, Jarvis and Amenzo, a short distance below the mill.

Mr. Baker being of an amicable and docile temperament, he was often selected as a trusty by his father, who could always depend upon his integrity.

In 1839 he removed with his parents to Lee County, Iowa. This journey was made via the Niagara Falls, crossing the river in a boat about ten miles below the falls, and thence to Kirtland, Ohio, visiting the Latter-day Saints Temple, continued their journey to the west, locating in Lee County, Iowa, near Montrose, in Ambrosure district. Here his father located a farm, but the disadvantages of a new country, a new home to make, farm to fence and land to prepare for planting. This, with a deficiency of clothing, scarcity of food, made life a struggle for existence. With these conditions no wonder his childhood days were not the smoothest; his chances for education or social advancement anything but encouraging.

Here on their farm in Lee County, his mother died, leaving a family of eight small children to care for. The marriage of his father to that noble woman, Charlotte Leavitt, five weeks later, who proved to be a good mother to those motherless children. This followed one year later by the expulsion of the Mormons from Nauvoo and vicinity; abandoning their home in Iowa, fleeing with the "Saints," they knew not whither, resting a few weeks on the east banks of the Missouri River, then crossing over and locating in that memorable town, Winter Quarters.

Here it was that on one occasion, his father, though of strong character, and schooled in the trials and privations of frontier life, experienced one of the most touching trials of his existence, that of his children crying for bread and none to be procured for their sustenance.

When in the spring of 1847 his father's family started on their westward march for the Rocky Mountains, he was placed in charge of three yoke of oxen and a wagon, and though shoeless and bareheaded, he was faithful to the task, driving this team 1,000 miles across plains and mountains, inhabited only by fierce savages and wild animals, and on to the borders of the Great Salt Lake, where they assisted in establishing the "City of the Saints."

On nearing the Rocky Mountains, they were met by President Brigham Young's Company, who were returning to Winter Quarters, the two companies camping together that night. On account of the visitors, the usual guard duty was omitted, so Albert took the precaution to stake a colt, which his father had given him, near the wagon, and during the night, the Indians made a raid on their herds, driving off so many of their mules and oxen that they were unable to continue their journey the next morning; but, Albert's pony, to which he was greatly attached, was to his great joy, secure in camp.

Continuing their journey, they arrived in Salt Lake City Oct. 2, 1847, where Albert assisted in herding and caring for the stock.

From 1851 to 1855 he worked in North Canyon, east of Bountiful, getting out timber for the Salt Lake Temple and other purposes, except during the winter of 1854, when he worked on the Jordan ranch, where his father had some 40 cows to milk and feed, making butter for the Salt Lake City market.

Mrs. Baker having returned to the city for the winter, his father secured the services of a Mrs. Curtis and her daughter, Jane Maria, to assist in the dairy work on the ranch. A few months later an attachment between Mr. Baker and Miss Curtis resulted in an engagement, which was followed by their marriage in December at Salt Lake City, returning to the ranch for the winter.

In August, 1855, he assisted his brother, George, in taking a herd of his father's stock to Cache Valley. He then returned and lived on the ranch during the winter of 1855-6 and the following spring, himself and wife, together with his father and others, went as colonists to Carson Valley, Nev., arriving there in July; leaving his father at this place, he took an ox team and some stock and moved over into Eagle Valley, where he located a ranch of 160 acres. Here he built a log house, a pole corral, put up some hay, and then made a trip to California with his father to procure supplies for the winter. After their return, his father having decided to go to Salt Lake City on a visit, ask Albert and his wife to come to his ranch for the winter and assist in caring for the farm and stock, so leaving their new home, they moved over to his father's ranch, and not returning to live on his own ranch again, he sold it for $5.00, the amount of the surveyor's fee.

In the spring of 1857 he moved to Warsaw Valley, bought a lot, intending to make another home, built a small log cabin, intending it for a chicken coop, but used it for a house; he also buullt a corral and put up some hay for winter. By this time, word came to them that Johnston's Army was approaching Utah, and advising all the Nevada "Saints" to return; so again abandoning their possessions, they with the returning company journeying back to Salt Lake City, arriving there in August, 1857.

There was considerable excitement at this time regarding the attitude of the United States Government towards the people of Utah, followed by the exodus of the people to the south in the spring of 1858. At first assisting in moving some of the poor families as far south as Provo, he in May started with his own outfit for Iron County, his wife driving the team, while he, assisted by Pete, an Indian boy, obtained in Nevada, followed with the stock. On this trip, when near Beaver Creek, they were met by a small band of Indian squaws and papooses, and on reaching the crossing, there was lined up on either side of the road about 20 Indian braves, with war paint on, and guns ready for action. Mr. Baker grasping the situation, knowing it was useless to run, instructed that brave little woman to drive on and pay no attention to the Indians. So she, undauntedly, drove the ox teams through this double line of savages, while he, having a hard time to keep his Indian boy from decamping, succeeded in driving the stock across the stream. The Indians, when they saw this bravery shown, modified their attitude and became friendly, saying: "Heap man, Ka squaw" (Big man—no woman), meaning, he was brave, not feint-hearted.

They arrived soon after at Paragoonah, Iron County, where he assisted his brother-in-law in putting up hay, and after the treaty with the United States Commissioners, they returned to Salt Lake City, arriving there in September, 1858, moving into the Porter house, owned by Abraham Coon.

In 1860 he, together with two of his brothers, Amenzo and George, moved to Cache Valley, for the purpose of locating new homes. Leaving Salt Lake City in April, they soon after located on Gardner Creek, a small stream between what is now Wellsville and Mendon, where a garden and some grain were planted that season.

George, Amenzo and the Indian boy lived with them, making a family of five, who for a time used their wagons to live in. Some time was spent by the Baker brothers in assisting the Mendon people in putting in an arrigation dam on Gardner Creek but being poorly planned, it soon washed away. Mr. Baker was then selected as foreman, taking charge of its reconstruction, the dam was rebuilt, and now, 50 years later, is secure and in good condition.

The Indians being troublesome, the Bakers moved to Mendon for protection, living in a dugout until a house could be built, which was soon completed in the Mendon fort.

During the winter of 1862 he, with others, herded stock owned by the Latter-day Saints Church and Cache Valley settlers, at the

Promotory range, about 30 miles west of Mendon, near the Great Salt Lake.

During the year of 1863 he went with one of the emigration companies from Utah to Florence, Neb., to assist in bringing aross the plains the emigrants of that season, covering about five months time for the round trip. Mr. Baker was selected and put in charge of the night herd by his captain, William B. Preston.

So well did he perform those important duties of night-guarding the stock, that when Captain Preston was asked to make another trip the following season, he refused to go unless Albert Baker would go also; remarking: "If I only knew that Albert was in camp, I could sleep; as all would go well." So Mr. Baker was chosen for a second expedition for 1864, being assigned the duty of assistant captain, having charge, not only of the night herd, but also of the camp, and assisting the captain in all things pertaining to the journey. It was difficult and perplexing to line up those emigrants for travel, some having never seen an ox team, and many of them speaking different languages.

While at Florence he was sent with some men and teams to transfer some freight from a boat on the Missouri River, and this being a rush order, through the excessive heat and over-exertion, Mr. Baker received a sunstroke from which he suffered for several days. On their westward trip they found the Platte River very high, the bridge gone, and found it necessary to travel some distance up the river before a ford could be found, and then, while most of the teams crossed in safety, some drifted into deep water, their wagons were upset, and it took several hours of cold and dangerous work in the water to get them out. When Albert arrived in camp, he was wet, tired and hungry. After securing and drinking some whisky, he, with his wet clothes on, rolled up in his buffalo robe for the night, and next morning was up and on duty as brisk as ever, while some others who had seemingly taken greater precautions, had bad colds, and were sick through the exposure of the previous day.

Mr. Baker, without renumeration, had spent two seasons on the plains, traveling 4,000 miles and assisting 1,000 people from Florence, Neb., to Utah, this last trip being his fifth trip across the plains with ox teams.

Soon after arriving home he was successful in moving his loghouse from the fort on his lot to the Mendon townsite and before winter was comfortably located in his new home.

He was captain of the minute men of Southern Cache Valley during the Indian troubles and at one time had a very narrow escape from an arrow shot from an Indian's bow as the Indian was concealed behind a willow fence. In the evening, just after going to bed, the dog began barking fiercely. Mr. Baker jumped out of bed and, without stopping to dress, ran out towards his stable, and while in a stooping attitude, setting the dog on what he supposed was wolves behind the fence, the arrow pierced his finger and striking the bone, glanced off, thus preventing its entering his body.

During the winter of 1864-5 Mr. Baker and wife were in better circumstances for home comforts and enjoyment than at any time since their marriage; having the best log house and owning one of the three only stoves in the town. During the bitter cold month of February, when General Conner and Major McGary passed through the town with a detachment of United States soldiers to subdue the Indians on Bear River, they were entertained by Mr. Baker and wife, and complimented them on their comfortable home in so new a country.

In the spring of 1865 Mr. Baker was selected as Captain of the Mendon militia. At this time in the valley the majority of the men in the different settlements were lined up under military discipline, meeting once a week for military practice, and once a year there was a general three days drill in sham battles and military tactics to prepare them for emergencies with the Indians.

Mr. Baker's military career was from 1865 to 1870, during which time he proved himself efficient and capable as an officer in military affairs, and when arrayed in his military costume and equipment and astride of his favorite war horse, "Zack," he commanded a better appearance than some of the generals of the United States Army.

In the summer of 1866 he commenced the erection of an eight-room, two-story rock house, the largest residence in the town at that time. This was a great undertaking for those early days; nails were $1 per pound, 8x10 glass 75 cents each and other building material in proportion. He was told by his neighbors that the house would bankrupt him, but by perseverance and determination, he was successful in completing the building in 1869, moving into it on July 24. This house was for a number of years the village hotel.

In 1870 Albert and his brother, George, located on a tract of land about two miles northwest of Mendon, and later Albert bought George's interest, thus securing in both claims 320 acres. The old log house was moved on the farm as a homestead residence. In 1880 they decided to make their home on the farm, living there most of the time for 25 years, during which time Mr. Baker and his sons were engaged in farming and stock raising.

In 1896 Mr. Baker and his wife Maria moved back into Mendon to spend the remainder of their days in quietness and comfort, but he was yet ambitious and spent much of his time in improving his lot and residence in Mendon. In May and June, 1909, Mr. Baker and his sister, Mrs. Betsie Topham, did considerable work in the Latter-day Saints' Temple at Logan, Utah. On Aug. 25, 1909, he had a paralytic stroke while working in his garden. He was carried to his house, where he lay unconscious for several days. He passed peacefully to the great beyond on the 3d day of September, surrounded by all of his family, who now survive him. He was buried in the Mendon cemetery Sept. 6, 1909.

Thus closed the eventful life of a man who was a benefactor to the commonwealth. As a public man, his labors were for the benefit of all, as well as for his religion, to which he was true and faithful to the last.

Albert Mowry Baker was one of the Utah pioneers of 1847. A pioneer and one of the founders of Mendon, Utah, where he helped to make the first streets and bridges and the canyon roads, protected its people from the Indians while they slept. Well can it be said of him: The world and its people, his family and friends, are all better off, through his having been on earth, and like one of old, "He, although being dead, Yet Speaketh."

Mrs. Jane Maria Baker's early life and school days were at Holbeach, becoming a member of the Latter Day Saints Church at 11 years of age, and at 16 she was employed at dairy and domestic work by well-to-do English farmers. In 1853, she, with her mother, Mrs. Sarah (Wright) Curtis, set sail for America on the sailing vessel, Galconda, which on the voyage became disabled by losing its masts in a storm. They were eight weeks on the water, arriving at New Orleans, thence up the Mississippi River to St. Louis, Mo., and four weeks later to Keokuk, Iowa, where they joined Appleton Harmon's ox train for the west, arriving at Salt Lake City Oct. 16, 1853.

During the winter she learned of the death of her father in England, who intended to emigrate to Utah the following May. She was a true and faithful wife and a benevolent woman to the sick and afflicted. In charity work she was an ardent worker. For eighteen years she was first counselor to Elizabeth Willie in the Mendon Ward Relief Society of the Latter-day Saints Church and was president of the same for twenty-two years, during which time she did a noble work in behalf of the poor and the needy. At the age of 76 years she is now (1911) living quietly and happily at their old family home at Mendon.

Mrs. Edna Jane (Coon) Baker was born while her father's family were making their temporary home in Pottawottamie County, Iowa, and came with them to Utah in 1850, arriving at Salt Lake City at the age of two years.

Her father, Abraham Coon, a "Pennsylvania Dutchman," was a cooper by trade; a man of genial disposition and great force of character; a friend of the poor, sharing his last crust with them when in need.

Miss Edna Jane, at the age of eight years, went with her parents on that memorable "Carson Valley Mission" in 1856, arriving at Carson Valley on July 1, and the next day July 2, 1856, her mother died, leaving her father with a family of four small children, as follows: Edna J., Isaac, Jacob and Mary, who was only a few weeks old.

When the mission was abandoned, she returned with her parents to Salt Lake City in 1857 and was with them at the time of the "Move South" in the spring of 1858, going as far south as Spanish

Fork, in Utah County, and returning to Salt Lake City the following June, they made their home at the Jordan River, near the White bridge.

She well remembers the incident of seeing Johnston's Army crossing the bridge, and of four of the officers coming to her father's house to buy vegetables, and of their paying one dollar in gold for two quarts of green peas, which she had assisted in shelling.

She lived with her parents at the Jordan farm and at West Mountain, now Garfield, until 1865, when she went to Mendon, Cache County, and soon afterwards became the wife of Mr. Baker.

Aunt Jane, as she is familiarly called, was of a genial and sympathetic nature, possessing much tact and judgment in nursing the sick, and did much in charity work for the benefit of humanity.

Mrs. Baker has for many years been an active member of the Latter-day Saints Relief Society of Mendon, Utah, where she now (1911) lives in the house built by her husband 42 years ago.

Children: By wife Edna Jane, all born at Mendon.
180 Jane Maria, b. May 8, 1867, m. Samuel G. Spencer. X
181 Albert Mowry, b. Aug. 10, 1869, m. Alice Barnes. X
182 Sarah Elizabeth, b. Feb. 6, 1872. X
183 Charles Henry, b. Nov. 15, 1874, m. Charlotte J. Ladle. X
184 Abraham Coon, b. July 11, 1878, m. Lolo Pratt. X
185 Laura, b. June 11, 1881, m. James Peter Jensen. X
186 Jesse Simon, b. Feb. 3, 1884.
187 Edna, b. June 2, 1888. X

GEORGE W. BAKER, SR. 123   AGNES (RICHARDS) BAKER 123

(123)

GEORGE WASHINGTON BAKER (son of Simon) was born Sept. 9, 1837, at Pomfret, Chautauqua County, New York, being with his parents in their travels from place to place in early life. (See Simon Baker Biography). On arrival at Florence, Neb., in the fall of 1846 he was afflicted with the scurvy, a disease which became epidemic that year in the colonies, and from which hundreds died. The cause was said to have been on account of bad water and scarcity of vegetables, having to live almost entirely on bread and meat. Being bed-fast all winter, expected to die at any moment, but as spring approached, he took a change for the better, and though crippled at first, he as time progressed, recovered good health.

His father having returned from Missouri with two wagons of provisions which were left on the opposite side of the river, and George, on his first trip out of the house after his illness, went with his father across the river for the wagons, and when they were loaded on the ferryboat, George was in one of them, and Jarvis, his brother, came to him and had him get in the other wagon, and thus he escaped death once more, for, after landing, as the oxen were pulling the wagons up the embankment, the wagon first occupied by Mr. Baker broke loose from the oxen and ran back, one wheel in the boat and the other in the river, which turned the wagon bed upside down with thirty sacks of flour lodged in the cover.

About the first of May, 1847, the family left Florence, and went over to Elkhorn River, where they soon organized into companies and started on their journey westward, and in crossing the plains they saw many herds of buffaloes, numbering many hundreds of thousands, his father killing many of them with what he called his "pistoloon." Mr. Baker, standing behind a sage brush, saw his father kill one of them.

On October 2, 1847, they arrived in Salt Lake City, and as the family were building and preparing for winter, Mr. Baker's time was mostly spent in herding stock during the following winter, having neither hat, shoes nor coat, but fortunately this winter of 1847-8 was a mild one.

In 1851 Mr. Baker went with his father to work for the church in a canyon called "Baker's Canyon" or North Canyon, southeast of Bountiful, Davis County, Utah. He assisted his father in getting out wood and timber until the fall of 1853, when he and his brother, Amenzo, were called on a mission to the Snake Indians, where he engaged in helping to build Fort Supply (now Robertson, Wyo.), and in studying the Indian language. In June, 1854, he returned to his father's home, where he engaged in caring for the stock and dairy work until August, 1855, when he went with his father's stock to Cache Valley, which was then uninhabited. He and his brother, Joseph, built the first house (a log cabin), in the Valley, and here he remained during "the hard winter" of 1855-6.

In May, 1856, when his father was called on the Carson Valley mission, Mr. Baker was left in charge of his father's farm on the Jordan River. Flour this year was very scarce, on account of the grasshopper famine of the previous year, but they had plenty of beef, potatoes and milk. This, together with two or three hundred pounds of wheat bran, which they sifted for fine bread and made coarse bread from the siftings, they managed to exist until fall, when Mr. Baker determined to profit by past experience, and bought a two-year supply of provisions.

The following season of 1857, Mr. Baker again took charge of the farm. This being a very dry season, he hired a man, and put up all the hay he could at home. He then went to Cache Valley, and put up 60 tons of hay there, intending to winter part of the stock in Cache Valley. On returning home in July, intending to return to Cache Valley with part of the stock, he was disappointed on learning that the Carson Mission was broken up. His father soon returning, their plans were changed.

The United States having sent an army of some 14,000 troops to

Utah, as they believed, to hang all the Mormon leaders. President Brigham Young, who was then governor of Utah, began making preparations to oppose the United States Army by calling out the militia of the territory. Mr. Baker enlisted and started from Salt Lake City on August 14, 1857, with a company fitted out as cavalry, under the command of Col. R. F. Burton, going about 400 miles east, on the Sweet Water, where they remained until the United States troops came in sight, when they began falling back before the troops until they came to the Pacific Springs, where they intended to give the enemy a surprise by stampeding their mules and leaving them on foot. Accordingly, about 1 a. m., they rushed into the herd of mules, whooping and yelling and shooting off their pistols, which frightened the camp and their mules, but they were disappointed on account of the mules all having long ropes dragging with them which prevented their running. They then retreated, riding until noon the next day. They camped on Green River, and while preparing dinner, the picket guard came in camp and reported six wagons of the enemy close at hand. This they believed to be a good chance for some booty, which they much needed.

These wagons were guarded by 26 soldiers and a band of 33 volunteers were called to capture the booty, Mr. Baker being one of them. They started out without their dinner, and overtook the wagons just as they were met by the main United States Army, which had made a forced march. They then made a hasty retreat, sending a messenger ahead to notify the camp. This stampeded the camp, who, having broken camp in disorder, retreated, and it was late the next morning when they overtook them. They then pitched camp and received a long delayed meal and a little rest, and then they resumed their march to Fort Bridger, where they found a camp of their troops with plenty of supplies. This being the headquarters for their division, they remained here to get the much needed rest for themselves and horses. Here, Mr. Baker, through fatigue and exposure, became sick. Having no shelter, and getting no better, about eight days later, he received a permit from the colonel to go up to Fort Supply, where he received shelter and care with his brother, Amenzo, who was living there at that time. Mr. Baker soon recovered, and reported for duty. By this time, there had been a post established at Fort Supply, so he remained there, occasionally going to Fort Bridger with grain for the troops. At one time, he alone, took 12 United States prisoners from Fort Bridger to Fort Supply, a distance of 12 miles.

They remained at Fort Supply six weeks, taking care of the crops which had been left by the people who had abandoned this settlement and gone to Salt Lake City.

About December 1 the pickets brought in word that the United States troops were marching for Bridger. This, though a false alarm, came near making another stampede, and proved disastrous to them, as they burned everything that would burn in Fort Bridger and Fort

Supply, consisting of all the grain and some fifty good houses, one grist mill, one saw mill, and one threshing machine. They then fell back to their headquarters at Echo Canyon. Mr. Baker helped to build Fort Supply in 1853 and helped to burn it in 1857.

When it was ascertained that the United States troops were not coming to Fort Bridger, their scouts again quartered at Fort Supply. Now, they felt sadly the need of the goods, houses and supplies they had burned, as they had neither shelter nor grain, but fortunately had cached some 500 bushels of potatoes, and while they were out of flour (their supplies not having arrived) their scouts had secured 500 head of the fat beef cattle belonging to Uncle Sam, thus having to subsist on potatoes and fat beef with no salt. As the enemy at this time, Dec. 10, 1857, showed no signs of activity, the officers concluded to give the boys who went out in August a furlough to go home, and Mr. Baker returned to his home in Salt Lake City, a distance of 113 miles, arriving there December 15. He remained home three days, when with a fresh horse, he returned to his company, which was a roaming scout, having no quarters, camping and sleeping anywhere night overtook them, not stopping more than two nights in a place, making their beds in the snow, cooking their food in the ashes (having no cooking utensils), remained on the borders of the enemy until the United States troops came up to Bridger and went into Winter Quarters. Then they fell back to Echo Canyon, where it was thought that a picket guard would be sufficient, so the troops were released to go home, arriving there in Salt Lake City, Dec. 26, 1857. Mr. Baker remained home a few days, then went to Cache Valley, where his father, during his absence (according to his original plan) had taken part of the stock there to winter. He remained there during the winter with his brother, Joseph, taking care of the stock until spring opened, so they could get the stock out of the valley; they took them back to their ranch on the Jordan and abandoned Cache Valley.

By this time, President Young had given orders for the people to leave their homes and move south, so accordingly, those who had teams had to move those who had no teams, and Mr. Baker in March and April made two or three trips with the poor before his father moved south with the family.

On returning from the "Move South" he assisted in putting up the hay on his father's ranch, and then about September 1 hired out to a Mr. Markley at $40.00 per month, to go to Sweetwater, 350 miles east of Salt Lake City, to build a stage station and put up hay for the same, returning home early in December. The following summer of 1859, he made a trip with a load of passengers for William S. Godbe from Salt Lake City to California, crossing the Sierra Nevada Mountains with their lofty pines 225 feet high, four times, returning to Salt Lake City the following December, and helped to care for the stock during the winter, and began to lay plans for locating a home for himself, so receiving from his father about 30 head of cattle, the off shoot from two heifer calves given him some ten years before, together with some money he had saved from his California trip, fitted out with team, wagon and farm utensils, and together with his brothers, Amenzo and Albert, started for Cache Valley on April 5, 1860, to look up and locate homes for themselves.

Encircling the valley, visiting all the new settlements, finding no opportunity to locate homes in them, and returning to Mendon, the Bishop, A. P. Shumway, having 60 acres of land not yet distributed, let the Baker boys have it, being a 20-acre farm for each of them, adjoining the outskirts of this town, on Gardner's Creek, about Midway between Mendon and Wellsville.

Having put in about eight acres of wheat, barley, corn and potatoes, they turned their attention to getting out fence and building material. The Indians becoming troublesome, they moved into the Mendon Fort for protection on July 23, 1860, joining with people there in their July 24th celebration the next day and evening, attending a dance in their hall on a ground floor, with but half a tallow candle for a light. This, their first season on the new farm, they put up 40 tons of hay, and raised 63 bushels of wheat, 24 bushels of barley and 25 bushels of potatoes.

On Jan. 18, 1861, Mr. Baker married Agnes, the daughter of John and Agnes (Hill) Richards. She was born Nov. 1, 1843, in Nauvoo, Ill.

In the spring of 1862, he bought 30 acres of land nearer town. Dividing this with his three brothers, they had seven and one-half acres each. During these two years they were troubled much with the Indians, who stole nearly all their horses.

Their first baby, George Washington, Jr., was born Oct. 9, 1862, and merchandise being scarce, Mr. Baker found it necessary to go to Salt Lake City, some 80 miles distant, to get clothing for the baby, thus under difficulties and danger they struggled along, but with that determination and perseverance, characteristic of the Bakers, he was soon comfortably located in his own home.

During the following year, 1863, they raised good crops, and in September Mr. Baker was called to go and help colonize Bear Lake Valley, being asked to sell all his possessions and fit out for the trip. He went to Salt Lake City and borrowed $75.00 of his father to fit out with, thus retaining his Mendon property, which he left in care of his brother, Albert. He was ready to start about Sept. 15. Taking his family with him, he moved over to Bear Lake Valley, some 68 miles and after arriving there, he learned that it was a fraudulent call, so he returned again to Mendon, arriving there Oct. 5, and found his father living in his house and bed-fast. Mr. Baker and family lived in his wagon for the time, and took their meals with his brother, Albert.

In the spring of 1864, the Baker brothers bought a farm at Mendon, 40 acres, for their father's family, and this year the townsite was laid out and the people moved out of the fort and located on their town lots, where, in 1865, they started orchards and permanent improvements. In 1866 he raised about 500 bushels of wheat and the following season built himself one of the most substantial houses of the town, hiring the masonry, but doing the carpenter work himself. During the next four or five years the grasshoppers came by the millions and destroyed most of their crops

About 1865 Mr. Baker was selected as a committee of one, to build a meeting house at Mendon, to levy a tax on the property and collect the same from the church members, to meet the expense of the building, which labor he performed with credit to himself and satisfaction to the entire community, and it is said the house he built was the best meeting house in the valley at that time.

In 1870, the town of Mendon received its charter, and became a corporate city, Mr. Baker being elected as its first mayor, in August of this year. As mayor he organized the city with a Board of Councilors, a force of police, a city marshal, recorder, prosecuting attorney, etc., and distributed the allotments to the citizens, issuing over 100 deeds, it is said, without one blunder or mistake. At the expiration of his term as mayor, he was elected Justice of the Peace, which office he held for two terms, ending in August, 1876.

In 1874, Mr. Baker was called to go to St. George to work on the Temple there. Leaving Cache Valley Nov. 11, 1874, he arrived in St. George. Some 450 miles south of Salt Lake City, on Nov. 28, assisting while there, part of the time cooking for the laborers, part of the time in the quarry, and helped to put up the walls of the temple. Receiving his discharge March 3, he started home on the 5th, arriving home March 16, 1875.

During the winter of 1876 Mr. Baker sold his comfortable home at Mendon, intending to emigrate to Arizona, but after receiving his money for the place, $1,500, he saw he had made a mistake, so bought a lot and farm again in Mendon, built on his new lot a comfortable home, where he now resides in comfort and plenty.

Children: All born at Mendon, Utah.
188 George Washington, b. Oct. 9, 1862, m. Orelia M. Atwood. X
189 Mary Emma, b. July 30, 1864, m. Jens Jensen. X
190 Julia, b. Aug. 3, 1866, m. Franklin R. Christenson. X
191 Joseph Albert, b. March 30, 1869, m. Alice H. Hinkle. X
192 Lucy Agnes, b. June 2, 1871, m. Charles A. Johnson. X
193 John Simon, b. June 9, 1873, d. Aug. 10, 1908. X
194 Willard, b. June 26, 1876, m. Lena Elizabeth Foster. X
195 Lyman, b. May 17, 1878, m. Edith Lant. X
196 Celestia, b. Sept. 1, 1881, m. William Howell. X
197 Olive, b. July 18, 1885, m. H. Sumner Hatch. X
198 Seth, b. Aug. 11, 1887. X

GOLDEN WEDDING ANNIVERSARY.

There occurred at Mendon, Utah, Jan. 18, 1911, a gathering of the children of Mr. and Mrs. George W. Baker, to commemorate the fiftieth anniversary of their marriage.

A time of good cheer and rejoicing was had, and appropriate presents were bestowed upon the worthy parents, who were both hale and hearty.

This is the first house built and owned by Geo. W. Baker, Sr., and is the house in which his father, Simon Baker, died Oct. 22, 1863. It is also the house in which Geo. W. Baker, Jr., and his sisters, Mary and Julia, were born. Built in 1861 at Mendon, Cache County, Utah. Mr. Geo. W. Baker sitting in the door.

JOSEPH BAKER 124

LUCY (PACK) BAKER 124   MARY A. (MORGAN) BAKER 124

(124)

JUDGE JOS. BAKER, son of Simon, was born Aug. 15, 1837, in or near Montrose, Lee County, Iowa, about four miles west of Nauvoo, Ill. At this place his mother died March 4, 1845. His father, after the death of his mother, married Charlotte Leavitt. During the exodus of the Mormons from Nauvoo, the family joined with them on their journey west, and spent the winter of 1846-7 at Winter Quarters, which is now Florence, Neb. In 1847, while he was scarcely eight years old, having neither hat nor shoes, he drove a yoke of bulls on the "Old seven-foot Cannon," most of the way, in crossing the plains to the Rocky Mountains. This Cannon, being the first cannon brought west of the Missouri River, is now kept as a relic in the Salt Lake Museum.

During the winter of 1847-8 he assisted his brothers in digging thistle roots, segos and wild onions for the family, it being their chief food at this time; flour being very scarce, all lived on "rations" from October until the following July, when grain was harvested, which was ground in a hand mill for the family use.

On December 10, 1850, he, together with his father and some 200 others, with teams, under the leadership of George A. Smith, left Salt Lake City for the purpose of colonizing Iron County and located Parawan, Utah.

The following spring of 1851 his father sold their location to John Topham, and he and his father returned to Salt Lake City.

His father at this time contracted with the church to haul timber and wood from the North Canyon east of Bountiful, called Baker's Canyon. Here he worked for four years, except during the winter, when he went on the ranch, west of Jordan River, near its mouth, where his father kept his cattle and horses during the winter.

Early in July, 1855, President Brigham Young, desiring to settle Cache Valley, invited his father, together with some other stock raisers to go to the valley and prepare to winter their stock there. On July 17 the following persons, as pioneers, left Salt Lake City for Cache Valley, arriving there on July 20, 1855. Bryant Stringham as captain, Simon Baker and Andrew Moffett, Councilors. These, together with Joseph Baker, Brigham Young, Jr., Thomas Clayton, Thomas Naylor, Thomas Kendall and George Twist, comprised the party of explorers. They first camped near where Wellsville is now located. The following day, July 21, Captain Stringham, Simon Baker, Young and Moffett, started on horseback to explore the valley to find the best location, and after three days riding they selected what is known as the Church Farm. While they were exploring the valley, Joseph Baker cut and hauled a load of poles and made a calf's pen, as they had two cows and calves along with them. This was at Haw Brush Springs, and was the first mark of civilization in Cache Valley.

After they had decided on their location, Mr. Stringham said: "Boys, I'm going to have the honor of cutting the first house log." Mr. Baker replied: "If you do, you will have to fall the tree on me." They each commenced chopping at the same tree. Mr. Baker was successful in reaching the heart of the tree first, and fell the tree on Stringham, thus securing the honor of cutting the first house log in the valley for himself.

About a month later his brothers, George W. and Albert M. came into the valley with a herd of cattle and horses. They cut and put up during this season about 40 tons of hay, and the following September Mr. Baker and his brother, George W., built on Church Farm the first cabin in the valley.

That memorable "hard winter" of 1856 came, with snow three and one-half feet deep all over the valley, which lasted from December until April 30. After removing all the cattle that could be driven out of the valley, Mr. Baker and eight other young men were left there to feed some 120 head of cattle that were left there. By April 1 they had used all their flour and bacon and their cattle were too poor for beef, and, fortunately at that time, the prairie chickens came by the thousands to their corral to roost and by getting up early in the morning they could shoot all they needed before breakfast, and having one bushel of seed wheat and half a bushel of seed peas, they had all the pea soup they cared for, so were living well when relief came in the spring.

On returning to Salt Lake City, he learned that at the General Conference held there April 6, 1856, his father had been called to go on a mission to colonize Carson Valley, so Mr. Baker concluded to go with them, and leaving Salt Lake City the latter part of May, together with a number of others, taking with them about 150 head of cattle and some horses, they arrived at Carson about the first of July, where his father bought a farm of 640 acres, paying in cattle and horses for the same. There on that location, called the Niles and Sears farm, was born to his father's wife, Elizabeth, a son, named James Staples, in honor of his maternal grandfather.

Early in December of this year his father, together with six others, started on a return trip to Salt Lake City, leaving him in charge of the place during his absence, which was until June 1, 1857, and on June 12, he and his father started over the Sierra Nevada Mountains for California, to find his brother Jarvis, who went there in 1850. They found him and he returned with them to Carson.

The latter part of July they started for Salt Lake City, the mission having been abandoned on account of the Echo War. They were 26 days making the trip to Salt Lake City, having found and buried a number of emigrants, whom Indians had killed while on their way to California. In the fall of 1857 he went to Cache Valley with part of his father's stock to winter, while his brothers took care of those on the Jordan ranch. In the spring of 1858 his father and brother, George, came and helped to move the stock to Salt Lake City, and soon after moved on south to Provo bottoms, where they remained until after the treaty of peace was concluded, June 10 to 12, 1858, between the United States Commissioners and the Mormon leaders.

They then returned to Salt Lake City, where he attended school during the following winter.

During the spring of 1859 he ranched and sold 500 head of oxen for H. C. Perry, a prominent merchant of Salt Lake City.

On July 10, 1859, he was married to Lucy Amelia Pack, by Brigham Young, which proved to be a happy union. They resided in Salt Lake City until the following spring, when they removed to South Bountiful, where they lived until the spring of 1861, when they removed to Mendon, Cache Valley. He joined his brothers, Amenzo, Albert and George W., who settled there the preceding year. They divided their land with him, which gave them 15 acres each. They afterwards bought 30 acres more and divided it equally between the four Baker brothers. At this time the Indians were very hostile, stealing their horses and cattle; his time was mostly taken up with guard duty, or, chasing those that stole their stock; being a minute man, he was on duty most of the time for three years, until General Conner came up from Fort Douglas, with a detachment of soldiers and killed about 300 Indians, which made "Good Indians" of them.

In the spring of 1864 the people moved out of their Log Fort onto their town lots, Mr. Baker building first a log house on the lot where he now lives, and two years later, 1866, he commenced building a stone house, completing it 1867. This was the first stone house built in Mendon.

All seemed well and happy with them until Aug. 10, 1873, when they lost by death their youngest son, George Eaton. Mrs. Baker seemed heart broken, and was sick from that time until her death, April 16, 1874, leaving Mr. Baker with eight small children to care for. Mr. Baker referring to the sad occurrence, said: "I felt that I would die with grief; but God tempers the breeze to the shorn lamb, and I saw in a dream, the woman that was to take her place, although she was in Wales at the time, I knew her when I first saw her, and on July 26, 1875, she became my wife."

Mr. Baker was married July 10, 1859, at Salt Lake City by President Brigham Young to Lucy Amelia, daughter of John and Lucy (Ives) Pack, a Utah pioneer of 1847. She was born June 22, 1837, at Kirtland, Ohio, and died April 16, 1874, at Mendon, Utah. He married second, July 26, 1875, at Salt Lake City, by Daniel H. Wells, Mary Alice, daughter of Thomas and Ann (Roberts) Morgan. She was born March 6, 1855, at Merthyr, Glamorganshire, South Wales.

He has held many offices of trust in his home town and is now (1910) Justice of the Peace there.

Children: All born in Mendon, except the first and last named.
199 Joseph Lindon, b. March 22, 1860, in Salt Lake City, d. Jan. 10, 1880, at Mendon.
200 Jesse Merrit, b. Nov. 11, 1861, m. Sarah A. Dowdle. X
201 Simon Pack, b. Jan. 3, 1864, m. Sarah Bassett. X
202 John Rupert, b. Nov. 29, 1865, m. Sarah Bassett. X
203 Lucy Amelia, b. Oct. 22, 1867, m. Albert W. Raybold. X

204 Charlotte Eleanor, June 16, 1869, m. David T. Owens. X
205 Tamsan Louella, b. Feb. 23, 1871, m. Edgar Arlington. X
206 Ward Eaton, b. Jan. 15, 1873, d. Aug. 10, 1873.
207 George Caleb, b. April 10, 1874, d. April 10, 1874, aged 2 hours.
  Children: By second wife.
208 Mary Elizabeth, b. April 28, 1876, d. Feb. 22, 1877.
209 Thomas Morgan, b. March 27, 1877.
210 Albert Marvin, b. June 20, 1879.
211 Richard Morgan, b. Dec. 24, 1880.
212 Annie Maria, b. Oct. 30, 1882.
213 Alice, b. March 20, 1884, m. Ferris E. Jones. X
214 David M., b. Nov. 2, 1885.
215 William Melvin, b. March 12, 1887.
216 Alma, b. June 12, 1889.
217 Florence Geneva, b. March 22, 1891, d. April 16, 1896.
218 Hazel May, b. May 30, 1893.
219 Margaret Edna, b. Oct. 7, 1895, d. Nov. 25, 1909.
220 Mary Geneva Morris, b. Sept. 23, 1901, at Brigham City, Utah, adopted daughter of Mrs. Baker's sister, Elizabeth Morris.

(129)

BENJAMIN BAKER was born July 6, 1847, at Dog Town, Pawnee County, Nebraska. Married first December, 1873, at Salt Lake City, Utah, Margaret Ann, daughter of William and Elizabeth (Murdock) Rowe. She was born March 19, 1856, at Parawan, Utah. She, while driving a team across the railroad, was thrown from the track by an engine on a passing train and died from the effects of the accident on March 30, 1884, at Lewiston, Utah.

Mr. Baker married second Oct. 14, 1887, at Mendon, Cache County, Utah, Lucy, daughter of George and Mary (Moulder) Goatman. She was born Oct. 16, 1859, at Glostershire, England.

Mr. Baker was born while the family were emigrating to the Rocky Mountains, and it is said there was no delay occasioned by his birth, as the family continued daily on the journey.

Mr. Baker soon after marriage located at Lewiston, Utah, where he resided until about 1885, when he removed to Teton, Idaho. Returning to Lewiston about 1890, he resided there until 1899, when he removed to Leavitt, Alta, Canada, where they now (1910) reside.

Children: By first wife, Margaret A.
221 Levi, b. Jan. 28, 1875, at Lewiston, Utah, m. Emma Webster. X
222 Lottie Margaret, b. June 7, 1877, at Lewiston, m. Samuel H. Self. X.
223 Elizabeth Ann, b. Nov. 2, 1879, at Lewiston, Utah, d. Sept. 21, 1882, at Franklin, Idaho.
224 Bennie, b. Jan. 28, 1883, at Franklin, Idaho, d. Aug. 20, 1883, at Mendon, Utah.

Children: By second wife, Lucy.
225 Benjamin George, b. July 22, 1888, at Teton, Idaho.
226 Mary Ann, b. Feb. 25, 1890.
227 Joseph Henry, b. Sept. 21, 1891, at Lewiston, Utah.
228 Esther Emma, b. June 6, 1893, at Lewiston, Utah.
229 Rose, b. Dec. 21, 1895, at Lewiston, Utah.
230 Simon, b. Jan. 30, 1896, at Salt River Valley.
231 Phoebe, b. Sept. 13, 1898, at Lewiston, Utah.
232 Martha Abigail, b. June 10, 1900, at Leavitt, Canada.
233 Sarah, b. Feb. 20, 1902, at Leavitt, Alta, Canada.
234 Evaline, b. June 19, 1904, at Leavitt, Alberta, Canada.

WIEAR BAKER 133   ELECTA (HAWS) BAKER 133

(133)

WIEAR BAKER (son of Simon) was born July 20, 1854, in Salt Lake City, Utah. Removed with his mother during the spring of 1864 to Mendon, Utah, where he resided until 1885 when he located on a ranch at Teton, Idaho, this being his present place of residence. He married Nov. 24, 1892, at Teton, Idaho, Electa, daughter of Geo. W. and Elizabeth A. (Worsley) Haws. She was born December 14, 1874, and died Oct. 12, 1904, at Pocatello, Idaho. Mr. Baker is Mormon in religion, Democrat in politics and is an extensive farmer and stock raiser.

Children: All born in Teton.

235 Stanley, b. Jan. 19, 1891.
236 Florence, b. July 28, 1894.
237 Clinton, b. Oct. 23, 1897.

FAMILY OF SAMUEL L. BAKER, SR.

1—Esther (Baker) Lynds 242. 2—Annie L. (Baker) Matkin 241. 3—Charlotte (Baker) Olsen 240. 4—Mildred (Baker) Matkin 238. 5—Martha (Baker) Leishman 239. 6—Mary Baker 243. 7—Samuel L. Baker, Jr. 244. 8—Alice Baker 246. 9—Annie (Leavitt) Baker 134. 10—Hattie Baker 248. 11—Samuel L. Baker, Sr. 134. 12—Zina Baker 247. 13—Phoebe Baker 245.

(134)

SAMUEL LEAVITT BAKER was born June 26, 1856, at Salt Lake City. Married Sept. 18, 1876, at Salt Lake City, Ann Eliza, daughter of Thomas Rowell and Ann Eliza (Jenkins) Leavitt. She was born Feb. 9, 1858, at Wellsville, Cache County, Utah.

They resided in Mendon after marriage until May 21, 1890, when they started on their trip for Canada. Leaving their Cache Valley home, driving their horses and cattle, hauling their seeds, household furniture, provisions, etc., the trip being one of many pleasant incidents, as fishing and hunting and a continuous change of scenery, their interest increased, as their dear old home would be farther behind as each night would close in, the evenings being spent in song, story telling, etc. At Eagle Rock (now Idaho Falls), they were met by Mrs. Baker's father, T. R. Leavitt, who came from Alberta, Canada, to meet his family and pilot them through. His knowledge of the camping grounds and his congenial spirit made for all a most pleasant journey, indeed, we might say a pleasure trip.

Arriving at the Dominion's Customs Office, their company was inspected, and proving satisfactory, were permitted to pass on. They arrived at Cardston July 8, somewhat seedy, but delighted with their surroundings, locating there, they proceeded to make a home.

He bought 160 acres of land from the railway company in the Buffalo Flat (better known as Leavitt), but resided in Cardston until October, 1896, when he sold out there and moved on to his farm at Leavitt, where today (1910) you may find Samuel L. Baker, prospering financially and spiritually, taking an active part in ecclesiastical affairs. He performed the duties of ward teacher for ten years, and afterwards became first councilor in the Second Quorum of Elders, living and helping others to live a Christian life.

Children:

238 Mildred, b. July 17, 1877, at Wellsville, Utah, m. Henry Matkin. X.
239 Martha, b. May 5, 1879, at Mendon, Utah, m. Joseph McKay Lieshman. X
240 Charlotte, b. March 21, 1881, at Mendon, Utah, m. Olif Albert Olsen. X
241 Annie Leavitt, b. Aug. 23, 1883, at Mendon, Utah, m. Simpson Arthur Matkin. X
242 Alta Esther, b. Nov. 28, 1886, at Mendon, Utah, m. James Lawrence Lynds. X
243 Mary, b. March 31, 1888, at Mendon, Utah.
244 Samuel, Jr., b. Oct. 17, 1891, at Cardston, Alta, Canada.
245 Phoebe, b. April 6, 1894, at Cardston, Alta, Canada.
246 Alice, b. July 14, 1897, at Cardston, Alta, Canada.
247 Zina, b. Dec. 24, 1899, at Leavitt, Alberta, Canada.
248 Hattie, b. June 6, 1903, at Leavitt, Alberta, Canada.

FAMILY OF JEREMIAH BAKER, SR.
1—Jeremiah Baker, Jr. 249. 2—Myrtle Baker 251. 3—Jeremiah Baker, Sr. 136. 4—Melvina E. Baker 253. 5—Mary T. (Lemon) Baker 136. 6—Vira Baker 252. 7—LeRoy Baker 250.

(136)

JEREMIAH BAKER, son of Simon, was born June 18, 1860, at Salt Lake City. He married Nov. 3, 1881, at Salt Lake City, Utah, Mary T, daughter of Jasper and Charlotte Melvina (Rawlins) Lemon, born Dec. 17, 1862, at Mendon, Utah. Politics, Republican, religion, Mormon.

Children: Born at Mendon, Utah.

249 Jeremiah, b. Dec. 5, 1882.
250 LeRoy, b. April 16, 1885, m. Charlotte Barrett. X
251 Myrtle, b. March 29, 1889.
252 Vira, b. April 15, 1891.
253 Melvina E., b. Dec. 7, 1894.

JAMES S. BAKER 138   ELIZABETH (CUNNINGHAM) BAKER 138

(138)

JAMES STAPLES BAKER, son of Simon and Elizabeth (Staples) Baker, was born at Genoa, Douglas County, Carson Valley, Nevada, Aug. 25, 1856, on the Niles and Sears farm, which his father bought when he went there to colonize Carson Valley. He married first July 1, 1878, at Salt Lake City, Utah, Louisa, daughter of Richard and Louisa (Field) Staples. She was born Nov. 13, 1857, at Birmingham, England; died April 28, 1883, at Salt Lake City, Utah. He was married second Sept. 24, 1884, at Market Lake, Idaho, by Merlin J. Stone, J. P., to Elizabeth, daughter of George and Elizabeth (McBride) Cunningham. She was born June 2, 1866, at Salt Lake City, Utah.

Mr. Baker's father having died when he was but seven years old, his opportunities for schooling were not the best. Much of the time he was the main support for his mother. In 1876 he went to Richmond, Cache County, Utah, bought a small farm, built a cabin and worked there at farming until 1879, when he entered the employ of the Hendricks Company as foreman on construction work in building the Utah and Northern Railway from Franklin to Beaver Canyon, Idaho.

He later worked two or three years in Montana and in March, 1883, he accepted a position with the Utah and Northern Railway as section foreman at Williams Junction, Mont., and has worked almost continuously since as section foreman, on the various railroads of Idaho, Utah, Wyoming, Nevada and California and is now (1910) filling the same position at Keene, Kern County, California.

Children: By first wife, Louisa.
254 Laura Louisa, b. Aug. 5, 1880, at Franklin, Idaho, d. June 23, 1884, at Ogden, Utah. X
255 James Richard, b. Jan. 1, 1883, at Morgan, Utah, d. July, 1883, at Ogden.

Children: By second wife, Elizabeth.
256 George Simon, b. April 2, 1886, at Ogden, Utah. X
257 John Henry, b. Jan. 8, 1888, at Pocatello, Idaho, d. there Feb. 1, 1888.
258 William Richard, b. Sept. 21, 1889, at Pocatello, Idaho. X
259 Ruth, b. Jan. 17, 1892, at Beckwith, Wyo. X
260 Mabel, b. Sept. 6, 1894, at Clarks, Nev., d. there Oct. 23, 1894.
261 Blanche, b. Sept. 21, 1895, at Lovelocks, Nev. X
262 Walter, b. May 8, 1899, at Ogden, Utah. X

HENRY BAKER 142　　　ISABEL (DENNETT) BAKER 142

(142)

HENRY BAKER, son of Simon and Ann (Staples) Baker, was born Jan. 2, 1858, at Salt Lake City. When a young man he removed with his mother to Mesa, Ariz., where he married Isabel Dennett. She was born Jan. 20, 1873, and died Dec. 26, 1903. Mr. Baker resides at this time in Mesa, his aged mother living with him.
　Children:
263 Nina Belle, b. May 5, 1903, in Mesa, Ariz.

JARVIS A. BAKER 161

(161)

JARVIS ALEXANDER BAKER was born April 18, 1867, at Mendon, Utah; married Oct. 2, 1890, at Baker City, Oregon, Pauline Pefferle. She was born Feb. 26, 1870, at Boise, Idaho.

Mr. Baker having had but limited advantages of the public schools at that early stage of Mendon's history, we find him at the age of 16 going to Ross' Fork, Idaho, to earn money with which to help bear his expenses at college. Here he worked during the summer of 1883, and entered the Brigham Young College at the commencement of the school year. The following year, 1884, was also spent at school.

In the fall of 1885 he engaged in mining at Alma, Wyoming, and in 1886 he entered the train service of the Union Pacific Railway, at Green River, Wyo. He was soon promoted to conductor, and in this capacity he has labored to the present time, working in the states of Wyoming, Idaho, Oregon, Washington, Montana, Colorado and Utah.

January 18, 1907, he had orders to take an extra train to Park City to assist in a wreck and while there received word that his youngest brother, Chester, had died that morning in the Park City hospital. It was fortunate that he was there at this critical time, to oversee the preparation of the body, and take it to their home at Mendon. It seems a singular occurrence that his three brothers should die while away, alone and among strangers, and that he and his brothers, John and Simon, should each bring one of the dead bodies home.

At present he is a conductor on the Denver & Rio Grande Railway, running between Salt Lake City and Helper, where he has been employed for the last five years.

Children:
264 Rena Rachel, b. Dec. 4, 1891, at Baker City, Oregon. X
265 Nina, b. July 20, 1893, at Ellenburg, Wash., m. July 2, 1910. X
266 Percy Jarvis, b. June 4, 1899, at La Grande, Ore., d. March 15, 1901, at Salida, Colo. X
267 LeRoy Pefferle, b. Aug. 12, 1905, at La Grande, Ore. X

JOHN D. BAKER 165
(165)

JOHN DANIEL BAKER was born March 26, 1877, at Mendon, Utah. His father died when he was fourteen years old and he was the oldest boy left at home to resume the responsibility of managing a farm and helping to care for a large family. He attended the public schools of Mendon and Logan and also the B. Y. college at Logan, Utah, during the years of 1897, 1899 and 1902, and in 1905 he attended the Latter-day Saints' University at Salt Lake City, Utah. Most of his time was spent on the farm; two years, however, he was engaged in shearing sheep in the shearing sections of Utah, Idaho, Nevada, California, Oregon and Montana. During two years beginning in November, 1903, he was in the train service of the Southern Pacific and Union Pacific railroads at Ogden, Utah, and the Great Northern railroad at Great Falls, Mont.

He was in Salt Lake City at the time of the death of his brother, Hyrum, at North Dakota, and met the remains at Butte and brought them home for burial. Later he went to St. Paul, Minn., and settled a claim in behalf of his mother for the death of her son, Hyrum.

He was called to fill a mission in the Central States, which he began Jan. 3, 1906, and labored in the states of Kansas and Missouri.

Feb. 25, 1907, he was sent with other elders to Independence, Mo., to prepare for the removal of the Missouri office, which was then at Kansas City. This was the first official move in returning to the Center Stake of Zion. He was appointed conference president over the St. John Conference, Kansas, Aug. 26, 1907, at which he labored until he was released June 22, 1908. At present he is engaged in farming and stock-raising at Mendon, Utah, and Southern Idaho.

SIMON M. BAKER 168
(168)

SIMON MORONI BAKER was born April 16, 1882, at Mendon, Utah. His early schooling was received with difficulties, attending the public schools of Mendon and Logan as opportunity presented itself.

During the years of 1899 and 1900 he attended the Brigham Young College at Logan and was engaged in various manual labors during the two years that followed. During the two years of 1902 and 1903 he was a student at the Utah Agricutulral College, where he took a course in Mechanic Arts, which has been of practical value to him since. He was of an athletic nature, and gained much skill in the football game with the college team.

At the time of his brother Asa's death, who was lost in the mountains, after a search of two days, he, accompanied by his cousins, Marvin and Jesse Baker, discovered the dead body and brought it home. This was a severe blow to him, as the two boys were constant companions.

He is now (1910) engaged in farming and stock-raising at Mendon, Utah, and Southern Idaho.

HYRUM LEROY BAKER 169

(169)

HYRUM LEROY BAKER was born March 27, 1885, on the Baker farm, near Mendon, Utah. He met his death in a railroad at Milton, North Dakota, Feb. 2, 1905.

During his life many accidents happened to him, and his life was many times despaired of. When a baby he came near losing his life from a severe attack of membranous croup and again from a long siege of scarlet fever. His right arm was broken when he was a baby and later when he was eleven years old, he fell from a granary porch and broke his left arm. He attended the public schools of Mendon and Logan. After completing the work prescribed for the public schools, he entered the Brigham Young College at Logan, and was a student there during the years of 1901 and 1902. Here, as in the public schools, he was an ambitious and industrious pupil. His efforts ever being crowned with success.

From his childhood he sought the companionship of his elders;

always taking greater pleasure in conversing with grown people than playing with the children. As a consequence his thoughts and actions were far in advance of his years.

When he was about 16 years old he went in company with his brother, John, to Idaho and Montana to shear sheep. He learned readily and soon became expert in his work. He also went in company with his brothers, John and Simon, two shearing seasons following this.

When through with his last shearing trip, he secured a position as brakeman on the Great Northern Railroad at Larimore, North Dakota. It was on this road a few months later, while discharging his duty that he met the fatal accident which terminated in his death.

The train on which he was breaking collided with a standing train just as they were entering the yards at Milton. There was a total wreck of the train; the track being torn up for hundreds of rods. There was a dense fog, and it was just getting dark when the accident happened. It was not until five hours later that his body was found, being buried in coal and cinders in the tender of the demolished engine. It is supposed that he was instantly killed. His body was received at Butte, Mont., by his brother John, who brought it home for interment.

He was generous, kind and ever thoughtful of his mother, contributing of his means for her support and that of the family. He was naturally of a charitable, manly and amiable disposition; qualities which gained him many friends. He maintained good habits and possessed physical endowments characteristic of his ancestors. Dr. Gibson, coroner at Langdon, North Dakota, after the examination, said that he was the most perfect type of physical manhood that he had ever seen.

An impressive funeral service was held in the Mendon meeting house, where the good habits and sterling qualities of the young man were eulogized by President Linford of the Brigham Young College, and other teachers and friends, after which the remains were buried in the Mendon cemetery.

ASA NORMAN BAKER 170

(170)

ASA NORMAN BAKER was born Thanksgiving Day, November 25, 1886, at the home of his grandfather, Richards, at Mendon, Cache County, Utah. He possessed a strong and healthy physique, was six feet two inches in height, proportionate in build and dark complexioned. From childhood he exhibited a helpful and unselfish disposition, always laboring for the interest of his mother, his sisters and his brothers. He grew up with an unselfish devotion for them, always sacrificing his own interests for their welfare. On one occasion, the day before Christmas, he traveled a distance of over ten miles to buy a Christmas present for his mother and for which he spent all the money he had saved for Christmas.

His education, like that of other members of the family, was obtained under difficulties, part of the time traveling from his home on the farm, a distance of three miles, every morning in order to get to school and back again at night. His greatest trial, however, when a child, was in being separated from his mother and home while attending school at Logan. After completing the course of study prescribed for the public schools, he was a student, 1904-1905, at the Utah Agricultural College at Logan, Utah. He became extremely interested in mechanics and won first place in the class of blacksmithing for skill and for the making of the numerous tools used in that profession.

One of his greatest pleasures was hunting. This amusement grew into an art with him and he became an expert marksman. It was while out hunting that he met his death. On the morning of December 4, 1905, while hunting deer in the mountains west of Mendon, he found a deer which he wounded and then followed, turning his horse loose, which seemed to prevent him from getting through the brush and up the steep mountain, he followed the deer on foot for three or four miles which brought him to the summit of the mountain. Here he gave up the chase and started home, taking the nearest and the easiest way, which was along the top of the mountain. From here he traveled about two miles toward his home. This course brought him to a point near the highest place on the mountain where the cold wind blew fiercest, and there through exposure and exhaustion, within five miles of his home, he perished in the snow. A searching party was organized, but was unsuccessful until the second day, when the body was discovered by his brother, Simon, who was accompanied by his cousins, Jesse and Marvin Baker.

The sorrow and grief which accompanied his death could be alleviated only by the inspiration and the nobility of his life; of his brightness of intellect, of his industry and self-denial, of his courage in times of adversity; characteristics which were hidden, but to those who intimately knew him.

Funeral services were held at Mendon and his remains were interred in the Mendon cemetery by the side of his brother, Hyrum.

NOAH CHESTER BAKER 171

(171)

NOAH CHESTER BAKER was born March 13, 1899, at Mendon, Cache County, Utah; died January 18, 1907, at Park City, Utah. He was seventeen years of age when he died, but he was well developed, five feet and eleven inches in height, and light complexioned; a type of vigorous and intelligent young manhood. He had a pleasant kind and tender disposition, combined with a strong will power.

He grew up, without the much-needed influence of a father, his father having died when he was two years of age. He was reared under the care of his mother, to whom he was always closely attached. His schooling, as that of his brother Asa's, was obtained under similar difficulties. He attended the public schools of Mendon and Logan and the Brigham Young College training school. After finishing the course of study prescribed for the public schools, he attended the

Utah Agricultural College at Logan, Utah, during the years of 1905 and 1906. While a student there in connection with his other studies he took advantage of the Art and Craft department, putting in all his leisure time and being quick to learn, he became skillful with the blacksmith's and with the carpenter's tools. The knowledge of which he afterwards put to good use in his work on the farm. He and his brother Asa were great friends and companions, and were very fond of each other.

After the deaths of his brothers, Hyrum and Asa, he was sad and lonely and concluded to go away from home for awhile to work. This being decided upon, about the middle of December, 1906, he went to Garfield, Utah, and secured employment there in the construction of a smelter. At this place he contracted a severe cold, so left the work, and went to Salt Lake City, where he stayed a short time with his sister Mercy. Before he had fully recovered from the cold he went to Park City, Utah, and secured employment in the Silver King Consolidated Mine. In this high altitude, and the mine in which he worked being damp and uncomfortable, his cold soon developed into pneumonia. He immediately went to the hospital. On arriving there his condition grew rapidly worse, and two days later he died, without any of his relatives knowing his condition till after his death.

His remains were taken to the home at Mendon by his brother, Jarvis, where beautiful and impressive funeral services were held, after which he was laid to rest by the side of his beloved brothers who had so lately preceded him.

AMENZO W. BAKER, JR. 172

(172)

AMENZO WHITE BAKER, JR., eldest son of the author of this genealogy, was born Nov. 3, 1865, at Mendon, Utah. He was single in 1911 and resides at Mendon.

HAMILTON S. BAKER 174

(174)

HAMILTON SIMON BAKER was born July 1, 1868, at Mendon, Utah; married there September 7, 1893, Christina, daughter of Abraham Sorenson. She died January, 1903, at Mendon, Utah.

He married second, October 19, 1904, at Mendon, Utah, Elizabeth, daughter of David and Agnes (Burnett) Buist.

Children: By first wife, born at Mendon.
268 Leslie, b. April 12, 1895.
269 Howard, b. September 4, 1896.
270 Ione, b. June 10, 1898.
271 Osmer, b. January 19, 1901.

ALEXANDER S. BAKER 177

(177)

ALEXANDER STEEL BAKER was born May 17, 1874, at Mendon, Utah, married June, 1894, Margerite Owena, daughter of Owen John and Frances Amelia (Godsel) Morgan. She was born October 11, 1875, at Salt Lake City, Utah.

Children:
272 Earl Morgan, b. April 25, 1895, at Mendon, Utah.
273 Alexander Stanley, b. July 10, 1898, at Mendon, Utah.
274 Ethel, b. Dec. 14, 1902, at Mercur, Utah.

ALBERT MOWRY BAKER, JR. 181 AND WIFE, ALICE (BARNES) BAKER 181

(181)

ALBERT MOWRY BAKER was born Aug. 10, 1869, at Mendon, Utah; married April 16, 1902, in the Latter-day Saints Temple at Logan, Utah, Alice, daughter of James and Lydia (Lund) Barnes. She was born January 23, 1876, at Ramsbottom, Lancashire, England.

Mr. Baker was the first child born in his father's two-story rock house, which was completed in 1869. His elementary schooling was received in the district schools at Mendon in the old rock meeting house, which was surrounded by a rock wall. He was a student at the B. Y. College in 1887-8 and again in 1890-91.

In 1892 Mr. Baker was appointed by his uncle, Amenzo W. Baker, to take charge of the Baker genealogical manuscripts (the original mss. of this volume) as they were at that date, with instructions to act as historian for the family and add thereto all additional records that he could secure, and during 1893-4 he assisted his uncle in his researches for more genealogical data, etc.

He filled a mission for the Latter-day Saints Church in the eastern states, 1894-6, leaving Salt Lake City April 14, 1894, and returning in July, 1896. While on this mission he visited many of the larger cities of the United States and Canada.

He also visited the historic and memorable "Cumorah", or Mormon Hill, situated about midway between Manchester and Palmyra, N. Y.

Mr. Baker on July 17, 1895, visited West Winfield, N. Y., the birth place of his grandfather and great-grandfather, Simon and Benjamin Baker; interviewed some of the older inhabitants, who were intimately acquainted with them; was shown the house owned by Benjamin Baker, in which Simon Baker was born; secured as a relic a maple pin used in the frame work of that house instead of nails, to hold the frame together. He also visited the cemetery where Benjamin Baker and others of his family were buried.

West Winfield, a town of about 800 inhabitants, situated on a small stream, has an academy with eight teachers; has four churches, Baptist, Catholic, Congregational and Methodist; has a system of water works, flagstone sidewalks, paved streets, etc.; has one bank, and also a tannery that employs about 50 men; has a flour mill, a planing mill, lumber yard, two hotels, Gold-cure Institute, etc.

Mr. Baker as custodian of the Baker records, in June, 1909, arranged with his uncle, Mr. Merlin J. Stone, of Ogden, Utah, to revise them for publication, and on Dec. 13, 1909, he was selected as one of a committee of three, together with his uncles, George W. and Joseph Baker, to devise ways and means for completing and printing the same.

Mr. Baker by occupation is a successful farmer and stock-raiser.

Children: Born at Mendon, Utah.
275 Albert Mowry, b. Jan. 23, 1903.
276 Irvin Lund, b. Nov. 23, 1904.
277 Asa Burdett, b. May 27, 1908.

SONS OF ALBERT MOWRY BAKER, JR. AND ALICE (BARNES) BAKER
1—Albert Mowry Baker 3rd 275. 2—Asa Burdette Baker 277. 3—Irvin Lund Baker 276

SONS OF ALBERT MOWRY BAKER, SR.
1—Abraham Coon Baker 184. 2—Jesse Simon Baker 186. 3—Albert Mowry Baker, Jr. 181. 4—Charles Henry Baker 183.

(183)

CHARLES HENRY BAKER was born Nov. 15, 1874, at Mendon, Utah; married June 14, 1899, at Logan, Utah, Charlotte Jane, daughter of John and Susanna (Trappett) Ladle. She was born June 22, 1880, at Farmington, Davis County, Utah.

Children: Born at Mendon, Utah.
278 Charles Duane, b. June 13, 1900.
279 Lucele, b. Feb. 9, 1902.
280 Merlin Albert, b. Oct. 5, 1903, d. Oct. 5, 1903.
281 Arva, b. Dec. 2, 1904.
282 Delone, b. June 16, 1907.
283 Horace Curtis, b. Nov. 10, 1909.

(184)

ABRAHAM COON BAKER was born July 11, 1878, at Mendon, Utah; married Nov. 15, 1907, in the Latter-day Saints Temple at Salt Lake City, Utah, Lola, daughter of Lorus Pratt, who was a son of Apostle Orson and Zina (Wheeler) Pratt. (Zina was the daughter of John G. Wheeler). Lola (Pratt) Baker was born March 14, 1889, at Salt Lake City, Utah.

Mr. Baker is a barber, learning his profession at the barber college at Salt Lake City. In June, 1908, he entered into the barber business at Logan, Utah, which place is his present residence.

Children:
284 Lola Anona, b. Nov. 1, 1908, at Logan, Utah.
284½ Abraham Clain, b. June 21, 1910, at Logan, Utah.

(186)

JESSE SIMON BAKER, son of Albert M. and Edna Jane (Coon) Baker, was born Feb. 3, 1884, at Mendon, Utah, where he received his early education and was graduated from the Mendon public school in 1901. In 1903-04 he attended the Brigham Young College at Logan, Utah, and in 1907 took the winter course of study at the same college.

He was the youngest son of the family and a great favorite of his father, his dicipline being left entirely to the discretion of his mother.

Mr. Baker is engaged in farming and stock-raising and at this time, 1911, is residing with his mother at Mendon.

GEO. W. BAKER, JR., M. D. 188

(188)

DR. GEORGE WASHINGTON BAKER, Jr. was born October 9, 1862, at Mendon, Utah; he married June 24, 1897, in the L. D. S. Temple at Salt Lake City, Utah; Oralie Melissa, daughter of William and Sarah Jane (Wade) Atwood; she was born Oct. 7, 1869, at Salt Lake City.

Mr. Baker, in his youth, was a very stirring and inquisitive child, learned to read and spell at home; entering the town school at the age of five years; he made rapid progress until he graduated; he then worked with his father on the farm.

At the age of 16 he worked for the Utah and Northern Railway, as a section hand, at $1.50 per day, saving what money he could, intending at some time to enter college, as he had a keen ambition for a higher education. The following year he went to Montana with a

Railroad grading company, with one of his father's teams, and cleared on the trip about $200.00. About this time the Brigham Young College was inaugurated at Logan, Utah, and in 1881, he entered the same, and after a two years' course in the College he acepted a position as school teacher at Franklin, Idaho. This position he held for two years.

In 1886 he was called to the missionary field, and filled a two years' mission in the state of Alabama, returning in 1888, when he accepted a position as school teacher at Deweyville, Utah, and the following year he was teacher at the North Ogden School, in Weber County. In 1890, he filled a position as salesman for W. H. Wright & Sons Co., at Ogden, Utah.

In 1891, after a short preparatory course with Dr. O. C. Ormsby, at Logan, Utah, he entered the Rush Medical College of Chicago, and after a three years' course he graduated with high honors, his diploma granting him the degree of Doctor of Medicine, etc.

During the College summer vacation of, 1892-93, he served as guard at the Columbian Exposition, and also served on the medical staff of the College Board of Health.

In 1893, returning to his home in Utah, he entered into a co-partnership with Dr. O. C. Ormsby, at Logan, Utah, where he commenced the practice of medicine; he did not, however, remain long with this firm, but began making preparations to open an office for himself. The sale of some real estate which he owned in Mendon enabled him to open up a respectable office in Ogden, Utah, the city of his choice in which to establish himself in his profession.

He later made several trips to Chicago, where he took further instruction in the later methods of Surgery and Medicine, thus keeping up to date in the medical profession, becoming one of the leading physicians of the city, having an extensive practice in the city, county and state.

In 1900 he was appointed by the State Board of Health, to canvass the state as Sanitary Inspector, which appointment he filled with credit to himself. In 1902, he was chosen as President of the State Medical Society of Utah, holding this position for two years, with great credit to the society. He is a prominent politician in the Democratic party of his home city..

Soon after marriage he bought a residence at 419 27th Street, Ogden, Utah, where he resided until December, 1910, when he bought a residence at 462 27th Street, where he now, 1911, resides.

Children: Born in Ogden, Utah.
285 George Lowell, b. June 3, 1899.
286 Oralie Virginia, b. Oct. 9, 1901.
287 Dorothy Aileen, b. Sept. 7, 1907.

JOSEPH ALBERT BAKER 191

(191)

JOSEPH ALBERT BAKER was born March 30, 1869, at Mendon, Utah; he married July 18, 1904, at Salt Lake City, Utah; Alice H. Hinkle Murphy.

During childhood he attended the District School at Mendon, Utah, supplementing his regular school studies with special courses while at work on the farm. In the early part of his 16th year, he went north to work on the Utah and Northern Railway, at Ross Fork, Idaho, returning home about two months later with a fractured collar bone.

In the fall of 1885 he entered the Brigham Young College, at

Logan, Utah, taking a two years' course, working during vacation each summer on his father's farm at Mendon.

In the fall of 1888, he entered the employ of the mercantile house of W. H. Wright & Sons Co., of Ogden, Utah. His inexperience in mercantile life compelled him to start in the lower positions. He rose rapidly, and in four years occupied a position first among the employees of the house. Excessive work during the first two years of this period induced a partial break down, which was closely followed by typhoid fever and pneumonia of a very serious nature, keeping him absent from business about five months. He emerged from this illness with weakened lungs, from which it took years to recover.

In 1892 he went to Pocatello, Idaho, and entered the employ of the Dry Goods House of Wiliam Bernstein & Co. After remaining with this firm for nearly two years he returned to Ogden, where he re-entered the employ of W. H. Wright & Sons Co., remaining with them until 1898, when he accepted a position with Walker Brothers Dry Goods Co., of Salt Lake City, where he served consecutively as Mail order manager, Floor manager, Assistant General manager and Buyer of women's ready to wear apparel.

In January, 1905, Mr. Baker and wife moved to Syracuse, N. Y., where he entered the mercantile house of D. McCarthy and Sons, under the management of S. V. Shelp, who, up to this time, had for years been general manager of Walker Bros. Dry Goods Co., of Salt Lake City, and through whose instrumentality this change of residence was affected. Anticipating the acquirement of a portion of the Capital Stock of the firm of D. McCarthy and Sons, the stock control of which it was expected would be in the hands of Mr. Shelp was the cause of Mr. Baker's move. Through an unexpected change of condition the stock acquirement was not affected, but, Mr. Baker remained as buyer and manager of women's and children's ready to wear goods under the general store management of Mr. Shelp, till the store was sold to another firm in 1906, when he and his wife moved to Columbus, Ohio, and he engaged as buyer and manager of women's and children's ready to wear departments of the mercantile house of The Morehouse Martiño Co., remaining with this firm till July, 1908, when, after a short residence in New York City, they removed to Seattle, Wash.

In Seattle, Mr. Baker was employed in the same capacity of buyer and manager of women's apparel in the firm of J. A. Baillargeon & Co., where he served till July, 1909, when he resigned and organized the firm of J. A. Baker & Co. of Seattle, Washington, with J. A. Baker as President and Manager and his wife, Alice H. Baker as Secretary and Treasurer.

During the greater part of twenty-two years of Mr. Baker's commercial life, he has kept up a systematic study and research along philosophical lines, following the apparently natural bent of his mind. Each move of Mr. Baker from one mercantile house to another was accompanied by financial advancement.

JOHN SIMON BAKER 193
(193)

JOHN SIMON BAKER was born June 9, 1873, at Mendon, Utah; at the age of five years he was stricken wtih a fever, which settled in his hip, leaving him lame for the remainder of his life. He attended the district school at Mendon until graduation. He afterwards remained on the farm, studying history and mathematics at a special school under Prof. Geo. Sorenson.

He entered the Agricultural College of Utah in 1895, and was graduated with high honors from that institution in 1899. During the vacations he worked on the U. S. Geological Survey with Prof. Baldwin and on the U. S. Hydrographic Survey with Prof. Fortier; he measured all the flowing waters of Utah.

Following his graduation he was elected County surveyor of Cache County, on the Democratic ticket, which position he held with credit for a term of two years.

During the early part of 1901, he went to Montana, where he was associated with Prof. Samuel Fortier of the Montana Agricultural College at Bozeman. He was later appointed professor of civil engineering in that institution; he resigned his position here to accept a position as Assistant State engineer and Secretary of the "Carey Land Act Board" at Helena, where he remained two years.

Leaving Helena, he went to Whitehall, Montana; here he opened an office and engaged in the promotion and development of numerous irrigation projects. Being particularly fitted for this work by his previous training, he met with unlimited success, and was overwhelmed with work. One of the projects which he undertook involved the irrigation of over 65,000 acres of land.

He also worked at Hydrographic and Topographic surveying in the department of the U. S. Geological Survey and became resident Hydrographer of Montana.

Late in July of 1908 he was stricken with diphtheria, from which he partially recovered, but the disease took a fatal turn and he passed away Aug. 10, 1908, at Whitehall. His body was shipped to Mendon, his old home, arriving August 13. Here his funeral was held on the lawn of his father's home; the services were very impressive. Prof. John T. Craine, Jr., of the U. A. C., Prof. Geo. Thomas also of the U. A. C. and Congressman Howell were the speakers. A quartette of his comrades rendered the music. His remains were consigned to their resting place in the Mendon Cemetery.

Mr. Baker was the possessor of a strong personality. Though afflicted by this physical disability which he was a very great obstacle in the active out door work of an engineer), he endured his afflictions without a murmur.

Hiss associates knew his generosity, admired his genial companionship and prized his royal gifts to them of professional knowledge.

As a student devoted to his duties, respectful to his instructors; as a teacher, enthusiastic, pains-taking and thoroughly informed; as an engineer, devoted to the best interests of the nation and state and thoroughly practical in every branch of the profession requiring his services; eminently successful in the development of natural resources; he took first rank among his brother engineers.

No member of the U. A. C. Alumni has met with greater success in his profession in so short a time; no one had a brighter future or greater prospect of serving his country and fellow men than Mr. Baker at the time of his sudden demise. Not only was he a servant to the pubic, but a devoted and affectionate friend. No one who knew him can ever forget his many sterling qualities, his energy, his precision and his dauntless ambition. As an evidence of his systematic mind may be mentioned the fact that he kept a diary from his graduation in June, 1899, until the day before his death with an entry for each day during that time.

He was a member of the Montana Society of Engineers and was recognized by all his fellow engineers as one of the foremost in the profession.

Mr. Baker was the possessor of rare ability in the musical line. He began his career as a musician while at home before entering college, being first a member of the Mendon band, under the leadership of Prof. R. L. Sweeten. After entering college he became a member of the college band and continued until graduation. During his connection with the Montana school he was instructor and leader of the college band and a church choir. He was a great student in science and literature; as an evidence of this he possessed a magnificient library.

WILLARD BAKER 194

(194)

WILLARD BAKER was born June 26, 1876, at Mendon, Utah. He married Feb. 16, 1907, at Anaconda, Montana, Lena Elizabeth daughter of Peter and Marguerette (Laird) Foster; she was born March 25, 1867, in Herkimer County, New York.

Mr. Baker, at the age of six, entered the District school at Mendon, Utah, and after graduation there, worked on his father's farm until 1895. He then entered the Agricultural, College at Logan Utah, and then after a three years' course at the College, he went to Anaconda, Montana, and worked with Mr. C. A. Johnson, his brother-in-law, in the electric works of the Anaconda Smelting Co. for a number of years. After his marriage he entered into the hotel busines at Anaconda, Montana, where he is now (1911) located.

LYMAN BAKER 195

(195)

LYMAN BAKER was born May 17, 1878, at Mendon, Utah; Married April 23, 1901; Edith Lant.

Mr. Baker first attended the District school of Mendon, Utah, and after graduation entered the Agricultural College at Logan, Utah, which he attended for two years and later took a course and graduated in scientific mining, and continues in that prafession at the present time; 1910.

Children:
288 Nettie Delorus, b, Jan. 27, 1902, at Silver City, Utah.
289 George Lant, b. April 28, 1903, at Payson City, Utah.
290 John Lyman, b. March 2, 1908, at Mercur City, Utah.

SETH BAKER 198

(198)

SETH BAKER was born Aug. 11, 1887, at Mendon, Utah, where he attended the District school and from which he graduated in 1903, and two years later entered the Brigham Young College, at Logan, Utah, and continued there the greater part of four wears. In September, 1908, he was stricken with typhoid fever, which kept him out of school for four months and greatly handicapped him in his college work. During the time he was at college, he was employed as band master and orchestra director, and played as also cornetist in the Logan Military Band; Jepperson's and Thatcher's Orchestras. He also played two years as first cornetist in Clive's Orchestra, at Wandamere, Salt Lake City.

He studied piano under Prof. Joseph F. Smith and harmony from Prof. U. C. Clive, and is at present cornetist at the Thatcher Opera House, at Logan, Utah. In 1910 he took up the composing and arrangement of music.

JESSE M. BAKER 200

(200)

JESSE MERRITT BAKER was born Nov. 11, 1861, at Mendon, Utah, where he resided during his boyhood days, workinng for his father until the spring of 1884, when he removed to the Snake River Valley, and located a farm in what is now Teton, Fremont County, Idaho, arriving there on April 22, 1884. On Aug. 17 following he was ordained High Priest of the L. D. S. Church, and set apart as Bishop's Councillor, which position he held until 1892, when he left his home and filled a two years' mission in Indiana, Illinois and Ohio, returning to his home in 1894.

He served 14 years as President of the Y. M. M. I. A. and for a number of years as President of the High Priests Quorum of Fremont Stake and is now High Councillor for the same. He is an extensive farmer, stock-raiser and dealer in general merchandise at Teton, Idaho.

He married Oct. 22, 1885, in the Latter Day Saints Temple at Logan, Utah, Sarah Ann, daughter of Robert and Henrietta (Messervy) Dowdle. She was born June 15, 1863, in Franklin, Oneida County, Idaho.

Children: All born at Teton, Idaho.
291 Jesse Alvin, b. Oct. 18, 1886.
292 Lucy Ada, b. Nov. 29, 1887.
293 Laura Henrietta, b. Dec. 15, 1889.
294 Louie May, b. Aug. 30, 1891.
295 Mary Lovier, b. June 6, 1895.
296 Lorin Merrit, b. March 13, 1897.
297 Doris, b. April 5, 1899.
298 Sarah Grace, b. April 21, 1901.
299 Harold Ray, b. Aug. 9, 1903.

SIMON PACK BAKER 201

(201)

SIMON PACK BAKER was born Jan. 3, 1864, at Mendon, Utah, where he married Oct. 3, 1884, Sarah, daughter of Thomas and Margaret Bassett; she was born April 1, 1865, at Canton, Glamorganshire, South Wales. Moved to Teton, 1885, where he was drowned July 9, 1888.

Children: born at Teton.
300 Ward Simon, b. Jan. 6, 1887.
301 Lucy Louella, b. March 10, 1889.

JOHN RUPERT BAKER 202

(202)

JOHN RUPERT BAKER was born Nov. 29, 1865, at Mendon, Utah, where he resided until 1885, when he removed to Teton, Idaho, where he married, December 23, 1890, Sarah (Bassett) Baker (widow of Simon P.). She was born April 1, 1865, at Glamorganshire, Wales.

Children: born at Teton.
302 Margaret Pearl, b. Feb. 26, 1892.
303 John Franklin, b. May 2, 1894.
304 Maude, b. Jan. 30, 1896.
305 Joseph Linden, b. May 13, 1898.
306 Estella, b. Aug. 24, 1900, d. Aug. 26, 1900, Teton.
307 Sarah Sedenia, b. Sep. 28, 1901, d. April 17, 1902, Teton.
308 Thomas Edward, b. April 29, 1903.
309 Maurine, b. Sept. 17, 1905, d. March 21, 1908, Teton.
310 Floyd Earl, b. Oct. 7, 1908.

SONS OF JOSEPH AND MARY A. (MORGAN) BAKER.
1—David Morgan Baker 214. 2—Alma Morgan Baker 216. 3—Albert Marvin Baker 210. 4—Thomas Morgan Baker 209. 5—Richard Morgan Baker 215. 6—William Melvin Baker 211.

(221)

LEVI BAKER was born Jan. 28, 1875, at Lewiston, Utah; married Oct. 26, 1907, at Auburn, Wyoming, Elen M., daughter of Samuel and Emma (Cleg) Webster; she was born March 21, 1890, at Rock Springs, Wyoming.

Children:

311 Albert Edward, b. Nov. 8, 1908, at Auburn, Wyoming.
312 Margaret Emma, b. March 7, 1910, at Tygee, Idaho.

Note—Samuel Webster was born Oct. 1, 1875, in England.
Emma (Cleg) Webster was born Oct. 21, 1873, at Bristol, Ind.

(250)

LEROY BAKER was born April 16, 1885, at Mendon, Utah; married Charlotte, daughter of William and Elizabeth (Wengren) Barrett. He died Aug. 24, 1907, at Mendon, Utah.

Children:

313 Le Roy, b. Sept. 29, 1907, at Mendon, Utah, died there April 10, 1908.

GEORGE BAKER 256.

(256)

GEORGE BAKER, son of James S. and Elizabeth (Cunningham) Baker, was born April 2, 1886, at Ogden, Utah. His education was received at the public schools while living with his parents.

Mr. Baker early entered the railway service. In 1902 and 1903 he was extra pumper for the Southern Pacific Co., at Kelton, Utah. In 1904 and 1905 he took charge of his father's farm near Lathrop, California. In 1906 he changed his occupation and worked at the carpenter trade in South San Francisco, California.

In 1907 he accepted a position with the Southern Pacific Co., in a student gang, on the Tehachapi Mountain. In 1909 he was section foreman at Edison, California, and in 1910 he had charge of a work-train and construction gang, distributing rails and material over the Tehachapi Mountains for the Southern Pacific Co., and later was section foreman over the Mojave yard and now, 1911, he holds the same position at Cameron, California.

WILLIAM R. BAKER 258

(258)

WILLIAM RICHARD BAKER, son of James S. and Elizabeth (Cunningham) Baker was born Sept. 21, 1889, at Pocatello, Idaho. His first schooling was at the age of seven, at Kelton, Utah, residing there with his parents until he was fourteen years old.

He removed with his parents, in 1903, to California, where his father bought a small ranch, at Lathrop, San Joquin County. The following year they removed to Ravenna, Los Angeles County, and a few months later to Acton, same county, where he was graduated from the grammar school, at the age of seventeen.

In 1906, he took charge of his father's ranch, at Lathrop, and the following year accepted a position with the S. P. R. R., at Caliente, California. On Nov. 25, 1908, he began work for the same company in the Signal Construction department, at Tehachapi, Kern County, California, putting in automatic signals and on May 17, 1909, he was promoted to a higher position and sent to Fresno, California; where he took charge of the Signal Station.

On June 25, 1909, he was transferred from Fresno to Edison, California, where he worked at the signal profession until May 19, 1910, when he was transferred to Caliente, California, his present location.

WALTER BAKER 262

(262)

WALTER BAKER, son of James S. and Elizabeth (Cunningham) Baker was born May 8, 1899, at Ogden, Utah. He now, 1911, resides with his parents, at Keene, California, where he this year completes his sixth grade at school.

PERCY JARVIS BAKER 266   LEROY P. BAKER 267

(266)

PERCY JARVIS BAKER, son of Jarvis A. and Pauline (Pefferle) Baker, was born June 4, 1899, at La Grande, Ore., and died March 15, 1901, at Salida, Colo.

(267)

LE ROY PEFFERLE BAKER, son of Jarvis A. and Pauline (Pefferle) Baker, was born Aug. 12, 1905, at La Grande, Ore.

THE LATE AMENZO W. BAKER.

MENDON.

ANOTHER PIONEER AT REST.

Amenzo W. Baker Closes Eventful Career At 75.

Special Correspondence.

Mendon, Cache Co., July 16.—Amenzo W. Baker, one of the 1847 pioneers, and a highly respected citizen of Cache county, died July 13, at his home in Mendon, Cache Co., of pneumonia. He was sick but six days. He was born in Herkimer county, N. Y., June 19, 1832, and gathered with his parents and the saints at Nauvoo in 1839. He lived at Montrose, Ia., up to the time of the expulsion of the saints from Nauvoo in 1846. He went to Winter Quarters, Ia., and in 1847 continued his journey with the saints to the valley of Salt Lake, arriving there in October of the same year. In the latter part of 1853 he was called to labor among the Indians and establish a mission at Fort Supply (Green River county), Wyo. Here he remained with several others under the leadership of John Nebeker until the invasion of Johnston's army in 1857, when the mission was abandoned. In 1860 he came to Mendon, Cache county, and engaged in farming which he followed until his demise. His wife preceded him three years. He is survived by four brothers and four sisters, all pioneers of 1847, also three sons and three daughters. He did much toward the developing of Utah, suffering many privations and hardships in the early days. He was a loyal citizen, a good Latter-day Saint, true to his convictions, a kind and accommodating neighbor and leaves a host of friends and relatives to mourn his departure.

The cut is from a recent photograph of the boy choir of the royal chapel at Madrid. On the day following the birth of the Prince of the Asturias the queen expressed a desire to hear these young singers, and they were stationed just outside the entrance to her apartments, where they sang several songs.

Keith-

Saturday will
of The Round-U

A shipment of Belts, intended for the Round-Up, but

The new lot contains 1712 belts, regular stock. . . . The biggest

Values to $4.45 Whit

Altogether it is a beautiful assortment of belts of patterns at real bargain prices. Of course, there will be 22, 24, 26, 28, 30 and 32. To avoid waiting get your rig

18 Belts—values $4.45............
456 Belts—values $3.00............
192 Belts—values $2.50............ **50c**
578 Belts—values $2.00............

REMNANTS HALF PRICE

PART SECOND

Baker Daughters and Their Descendants.

(34)

BENJAMIN HARRINGTON of North Kingston, R. I., married Sarah Baker.

Children:

314 Cyrus. X.

(45)

RANDALL MINER was born 1788, d. April 22, 1861; married Hannah Baker. She was born Feb. 19, 1793, at Leydon, Mass., and died Nov. 3, 1874. After death of her husband, she resided with her son Jerrah.

Children:

315 Laurinda, b. about 1811, d. 1870.
316 Benjamin R., b. 1813. Resided at Leydon, 1886.
317 Marilla, b. 1815, d. 1860.
318 Austin W., b. 1817. Resided in 1886, Springfield, Mass.
319 Emily, b. about 1818, d. 1850.
320 Norman B., b. about 1820, July, Guilford, Vt., d. Oct. 18, 1866.
321 Silas, b. 1822.
322 Lucy, b. 1824.
323 Lydia S., b. 1825.
324 Sibyl, b. 1827.
325 Jerrah, b. 1829, m. 1860, Caroline Brown. Four children. X
326 Emeline, b. 1832.
327 Ellen, b. 1838, d. May 29, 1858.

SHE FELL AT HER POST.

In Memory of Hannah Baker Miner.

(By Rev. W. A. Prof. Orange, Mass.)

Her trials all over, her sorrow all past,
Her long life of usefulness ended at last;
The master called for her, think not she is lost
For like a true soldier, she fell at her post.

For many long years, she a Christian had been,
Abhorring the very appearance of sin,
Contending with Satan and his wicked host,
Victorious her fall, she fell at her post.

She never retreated or turned from the fight,
But firmly contending in Jesus' own might
Her dear loved Savior sustaining the cost,
Of her Christian warfare, she fell at her post.

This mother in Israel now rests in deep sleep,
But you her dear offspring, why longer weep?
For at the command of the one she loved most,
She laid down her arms and fell at her post.

Like a ripe shock of corn, when the reaper has come,
She was tenderly gathered to her heaven her
Home no longer by tempest of time to be tossed,
Her warfare is ended. She fell at her post.

(46)

WM. HENRY SHEPARDSON (20) (See Shepardson Lineage) was born April 17, 1797, at Leydon, Mass. Died Aug. 31, 1846, Union County, Iowa. Married Jan. 23, 1823, Mary Baker. She was born Aug. 7, 1795, at Leydon, Mass., and died April 30, 1872, at Lions, Mills County, Iowa. They were baptized in the Latter Day Saint Church in 1843, by Elder Peletiah Brown. Came to Nauvoo in the spring of 1846. None of their children belonged to the Mormon Church.

Children:
328 Wm. Henry, b. Dec. 2, 1823, Colerain, Mass., d. 1904. Single.
329 Mary, b. Aug. 20, 1826, Colerain, Mass., m. Jonah M. Parsons. X.
330 Joseph, b. July 25, 1828, Leydon. X.
331 Lucinda, b. June 22, 1831, Leydon. Single.
332 Salome Rebecca, b. Aug. 4, 1834, Leydon.
333 Lydia Elizabeth, b. March 12, 1837, Norwich, Huron County, Ohio. X.

(54)

JOHN BROWN, of Hoosick, N. Y., married there Dec. 25, 1823, Esther, daughter of Jirah and Mary (Mosely) Baker. She was born Oct. 20, 1801.

Children: born at Hoosick.
334 Lucina, b. June 28, 1825.
335 Mary, b. June 5, 1828.
336 Susan, b. May 10, 1831.
337 Jonathan Mosely, b. May 8, 1833, d. June 11, 1834.
338 Sarah Esther, b. June 7, 1836.
339 Emily Augusta, b. Aug. 17, 1840, d. Aug. 16, 1841.

(56)

ARUNAH MOSELY, son of Arunah and Sarah (Shapeley) Mosely, was born April 4, 1801, at Lebanan, N. Y. Married Feb. 15, 1826, Mary, daughter of Jirah and Mary (Mosely) Baker. She was born May 17, 1805, at Hoosick, N. Y., and was the youngest daughter of her husband's first cousin. They settled at Lebanan, where he was Justice of the Peace.

In 1834 they moved to Ontario County, where he was again Justice of the Peace. They subsequently removed to Penfield, N. Y., where he was deacon in the Baptist Church. They afterwards removed to Perrington, N. Y., where he was again elected Justice of the Peace, and where they were living in 1856, in Fairport village.

Children:
340 Jirah, b. June 27, 1827, at Lebanan, m. May 19, 1853, Laura J. Ross.
341 Mary Elizabeth, b. Feb. 6, 1844; was living with her parents in 1856.

(63)

ELIJAH FERGUSON married Thankful Baker. She was born 1798.
Children:
342 James, d. y.
343 Mary, m.
344 Ira, d. y.

(74)

CAREY BURDICT was born Feb. 1, 1796, and died Jan. 4, 1854, in Mills County, Iowa. He married Mary Baker. She was born Feb. 10, 1801, at Hoosick, N. Y., and died March 24, 1872, Clitherall, Otter Tail County, Minnesota.
Children:
345 Oscar, d. killed in the war at the siege of Richmond, Va., under Gen. U. S. Grant.
346 Cabel, b. 1829. Resided near Sand Hills, Oswego County, N. Y.
347 Ann Janette, b. Feb. 18, 1831, m. F. L. Whiting. X.
348 Jackson. Resided at Clitherall, Minn.
349 Jesse, b. 1836.

(75)

EDWIN WATERS married Hannah Baker. She was born 1806 and died Nov. 25, 1851.
Children:
350 Edwin, died aged about 20.
351 Amanda Rebecca, m. Orrin Coleman. Resided in Ohio.

(76)

ELI W. MINER was born at Leydon, Mass., Jan. 15, 1816, and died at Hoosick Falls, N. Y., Feb. 15, 1851. He married Mary Baker. She was born Nov. 12, 1807, d. Aug. 21, 1874.
Children:
352 Sarah, m. Miner Brown. X.

(82)

J. EDWARD LOOMIS was born Aug. 7, 1815, in Connecticut. Came to Onandaga County, New York, 1817, and to Clay, N. Y., 1838, where he married Feb. 20, 1840, Mary A. Baker. She was born in 1820, in Lisander, N. Y. They settled at Clay, Onandaga County, New York, where they both were living in September, 1893.
Children:
353 Jennie, b. 1847, m. H. S. Van Wormer, of Phoenix, Oswego County, New York. X.
354 Jeffie, b. m. Josie Hoyt. X

(83)

JOHN McKELVEY was born Oct. 15, 1816, at Albany, N. Y. Went to Michigan when three years old, settled in Oakland County;

from there in 1833 to Lyons township, where he has since resided. He died of heart disease suddenly in his chair at Dexter house, on Saturday at midnight, 1893. Had been cheerful all evening and gave no sign of illness. For sixty years he had been a prominent figure in and about Ionie. Had many friends. He began to study law. when 30 years old. In 1843, at Lyons, Mich. he married Sarah Jane Baker. She was born May 18, 1822, in Clay, N. Y., and went to Michigan with her parents in 1840. They settled at Lyons, where she died Nov. 8, 1886. In later years, her physical afflictions were severe, but she thought life worth living, and when her summons came, she lay down as to pleasant dreams of a happy awakening.

Children:
355 Byron, lives at Boston township on a farm.
Three others, d. y.

(84)

REUBEN SMITH, m. Sept. 20, 1838, Mamie K. Baker.
Children:
356 Emily C., b. Oct. 21, 1839, m. Carlos Webster. X.
357 Mary M., b. April 22, 1842, unm.
358 Frank.
359 Augustus A.
360 Willie. X.

(88)

CHARLES E. RATHBUN married Feb. 2, 1848, Roxanna E. Baker. She was born Sept. 21, 1822, and was living in April, 1891.
Children:
361 C. Eugene, b. Dec. 12, 1849, m. Anna. X
362 William E., b. Feb. 23, 1852, unmarried.
363 Frank A., b. Aug. 28, 1854, m. Susie.

(92)

CHARLES O. KELLOG married July, 1850, Laura M. Baker. She was born July 25, 1831, and died April 9, 1886.
Children:
364 Frank L., b. Feb. 20, 1860, m. Christina and have one child, Mary Laura, b. Jan. 20, 1889.
365 Charles, b. May, 1852, d. February, 1853.

JOHN TOPHAM   BETSIE (BAKER) TOPHAM. 122

(122)

JOHN TOPHAM, son of John and Jane (Thornton) Topham, was born August 21, 1825, in the village of Honeydon, Parish of Eastonsocan, Bedfordshire, England; he married Dec. 3, 1850, at Salt Lake City, Utah, Betsie, daughter of Simon and Mercy (Young) Baker; she was born Jan. 24, 1835, at Pomfret, Chautauqua County, New York, came with her parents to Utah, driving an ox team, consisting of three yoke of cattle, across the plains, arriving in Salt Lake City, Oct. 2, 1847. Sharing in the trials and privations incident to its early settlement. On Dec. 10th, one week after marriage, they with a company of pioneers, under the leadership of President Geo. A. Smith, left Salt Lake City, to settle in Iron County, Utah, arriving at Center Creek, now known as Parawan, on Jan. 13, 1851. Here they resided for several years, again undergoing the hardships incident to the colonization of the Western Wilds; and later settling at Paragoonah, but on account of the Indian hostilities were forced to return to Parawan. In January, 1856, they removed to Paragoonah, where they made their home and have since resided, where Mr. Topham died Nov. 8, 1900.

    Children: First three born in Parawan; the rest born in Paragoonah.
366 James, b. Oct. 27, 1851, Parawan, died same day.
367 Charlotte E., b. Dec. 24, 1852, m. James Butler. X.
368 Mercy Jane, b. July 10, 1854, m. Ernest Samuel Horsely. X.
369 John Baker, b. Jan. 23, 1856, m. Mary Jane Barton. X.
370 Simon Thornton, b. Sept. 21, 1857, m. Alice Robinson. X.
371 Thomas Amenzo, b. Sept. 28, 1859, m. Annie Maria Lund.
372 George Albert, b. May 28, 1863, m. Laura Ellen Horsely. X.
373 Susan Adams, b. Sept. 28, 1865, m. Thomas Robinson. X.
374 William, b. July 18, 1868, died same day.
375 Joseph Riley, b. March 1, 1870, m. Harriet Isabelle Reynolds. X.
376 Hyrum Smith, b. April 21, 1872, d. March 15, 1873.
377 Silas Sanford, b. April 15, 1874, m. Amelia Jensen. X.

REBECCA (BAKER) JOHNSON 125
(125)

SNELLEN MARION JOHNSON, son of Willis and Nancy (Greer) Johnson, was born Oct. 27, 1827, in the state of Georgia. Married July 26, 1862, in Salt Lake City, Utah, Rebecca, daughter of Simon and Mercy (Young) Baker. She was born June 9, 1841, in Lee County, Iowa; came with her parents to Utah in 1847. Mr. Johnson died June 10, 1900, at Robertson, Uinta County, Wyoming, where most of his children are now located and where Mrs. Johnson yet resides.

Children:

378 Marion Nancy, b. Jan. 11, 1864, Springville, Utah, d. Sept. 21, 1867.
379 Thomas Irvin, b. Aug. 9, 1865, St. Charles, Idaho, m. Ida Bird. X
380 William Wallace, b. Feb. 5, 1867, St. Charles, Idaho, m. Alice M. Townsend. X.
381 Albert Marius, b. March 10, 1869, Lake Town, Utah, m. Alice Bird. X.
382 Joseph Amenzo, b. Aug. 18, 1871, Mendon, Utah, m. Maggie Baker. X.
383 Cora M., b. May 23, 1875, Lake Town, Utah, m. Solomon M. Hawkins. X.
384 Orville Deville, b. April 28, 1877, Randolph, Utah, d. Jan, 5, 1833. X.
385 Claude L., b. Feb. 19, 1879, Rock Springs, Wyo, m. Charlotte A. Baker. X.
386 Mercy Lenora, b. Jan. 15, 1881, at Lone Tree, Wyo., d. Jan. 5, 1883.

SARAH (BAKER) FARNSWORTH 127 AND HER GRAND-DAUGHTER,
GRACE CLARK 389

(127)

WILLIAM C. FARNSWORTH, born..;
died ....at Sacramento, California. He married..............
........................1863, at San Francisco, California, Sarah, daughter of Simon and Mercy (Young) Baker; she was born July 3, 1843, at or near Montrose, Lee County, Iowa.

Mrs. Farnsworth came with her father to the "Great Salt Lake" in 1847, arriving there on Oct. 2nd, and in 1861 she went with a family from Salt Lake City to California, and now, 1911, is residing at Sacramento.

Children: born at Sacramento.
387 Mercy, born at Sacramento.
388 Euclid, born at Sacramento.
389 Grace, born at Sacramento, m. Charles Clark. X.
390 a child, born at Sacramento, d. Sacramento.
391 a child, born at Sacramento, d. Sacramento.
392 a child, born at Sacramento, d. Sacramento.
393 a child, born at Sacramento, d. Sacramento.

(128)

THOMAS MATHEWS married June 17, 1865, in Salt Lake City, Utah, Abigail L., daughter of Simon and Charlotte (Leavitt) Baker. She was born Jan. 7, 1846, at Nauvoo, Ill. Came with her parents to Utah in 1847.

Children: All born in Salt Lake City.
394 Thomas W. Mathews, b. April 8, 1866, m. Annie Gray.   X
395 Charlotte Ann, b. Jan. 5, 1869, m. Miles R. Taylor.   X
396 Francis Marion, b. Dec. 10, 1869, m. Sarah Williams.   X
397 Mary Maud, b. Dec. 25, 1871, d. May 21, 1884.   X
398 Joseph Simon, b. Dec. 11, 1873, m. Bessie Ence.   X
399 Roy Baker, b. Nov. 25, 1875, m. Elizabeth Lawrence.   X

(130)

WILLIAM LONGSTROTH, son of Stephen and Anna (Guill) Longstroth, was born May 15, 1840, at Lancashire, England. Married Jan. 27, 1868, at Mendon, Utah, Charlotte, daughter of Simon and Charlotte (Leavitt) Baker. She was born April 5, 1849, at Salt Lake City, Utah.

Children: Born at Mendon, Utah.

400 Charlotte Ann, b. Nov. 12, 1868, m. Peter Larson. X
401 Stephen, b. Dec. 11, 1870, m. Leva Thomas Granger. X
402 Mary, b. Nov. 2, 1872, m. Thomas Muir. X
403 George Simon, b. Jan. 25, 1875.
404 Rosetta, b. Sept. 5, 1876, m. Fred J. Manning. X
405 Phoebe, b. Feb. 2, 1879, m. John W. Evans. X
406 Sarah, b. Feb. 18, 1882, m. James W. Wright. X
407 William Gill, b. Sept. 17, 1883, m. Clara May Sorenson. X
408 Allie, b. Dec. 21, 1885, m. Alfred T. Peterborg. X
409 Alma, b. June 7, 1888.
410 Ethel, b. Jan. 27, 1890.
411 Lymon, b. Dec. 28, 1892.

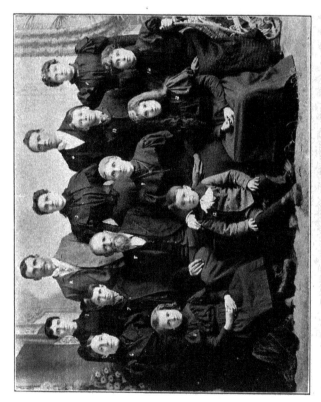

FAMILY OF WILLIAM LONGSTROTH 130

1—Mary (Longstroth) Muir 402. 2—Stephen Longstroth 401. 3—Rosette (Longstroth) Manning 404. 4—George S. Longstroth 403. 5—Phoebe (Longstroth) Evans 405. 6—Charlotte A. (Longstroth) Larson 400. 7—Alma Longstroth 409. 8—William Longstroth 130. 9—Charlotte (Baker) Longstroth 130. 10—William G. Longstroth 407. 11—Ethel Longstroth 410. 12—Lyman Longstroth 411. 13—Alice (Longstroth) Peterborg 408. 14—Sarah (Longstroth) Wright 406.

(135)

WILLIAM PETTIT WILLIE, son of James G. and Elizabeth (Pettit) Willie, was born July 12, 1848, at Salt Lake City, Utah. He married Jan. 6, 1881, in the Latter-Day Saints' Temple at Salt Lake City, Hannah, daughter of Simon and Charlotte (Leavitt) Baker. She was born Dec. 29, 1857, at Salt Lake City, Utah.

Mr. Willie's father, James Gray Willie, was the son of William Willie of Taunton, Sommersetshire, England, and was born at Taunton, where he resided until 21 years of age. He was a dry goods clerk at Taunton. At the age of 21 years he came to America and engaged in the government tanning business in New York City. He married there Elizabeth, daughter of William Pettit and came to Utah with same company that Simon Baker came with in 1847. In 1852 he went to England as missionary for the Latter-day Saints' Church, returning to Utah four years later, in 1856, crossing the plains with next to the last of the hand cart companies of that memorable "hand-cart" year.

Mr. Willie removed to Mendon, Cache County, Utah, with his parents, in 1859, where he now (1910) resides.

Children:
412 James Simon, b. Aug. 28, 1884, at Mendon, Utah.
413 George, b. Sept. 11, 1886, at Mendon, Utah.
414 Charlotte, b. March 26, 1888, at Washakie, Utah, d. Aug. 10, 1889, at Mendon.
415 Maude, b. July 29, 1892, at Preston, Idaho.
416 Sarah, b. Sept. 8, 1900, at Mendon, Utah.

SPENCER D. SHUMWAY   ELIZABETH (BAKER) SHUMWAY 139

(139)

SPENCER DAVID SHUMWAY, son of Charles and Henrietta (Bird) Shumway (see Shumway family, this volume), was born Oct. 23, 1855, in Little Cottonwood, Salt Lake County, Utah. In 1859 his parents moved to Wellsville, Cache County, and later moved to Mendon, where Mr. Shumway resided until 1877, when he removed to Richmond, Cache County. He married Oct. 23, 1877, at Logan, Utah, Elizabeth, daughter of Simon and Elizabeth (Staples) Baker. She was born July 8, 1858, in Salt Lake City, Utah, and at the time of her marriage was living at Richmond, Utah, where they resided about a year, when they removed to Johnson, Kane County, Utah. In the spring of 1881 they removed to Ogden, Utah, where Mr. Shumway worked during the summer and returned to Johnson again in the fall of 1881. In 1884 he removed to Taylor, Apache County, Arizona, where they resided until 1891, when they removed to Lindon, Navajo County, Arizona. Thence in 1898 to Mesa, Ariz., where they now (1910) reside.

Children:

417 Spencer Baker, b. Aug.-12, 1878, at Richmond, Utah, m. Annie L. Willis. X

418 Lydia, b. Aug. 18, 1880, at Johnson, Utah, d. there Dec. 29, 1882.

419 Henrietta, b. Nov. 30, 1882, Johnson, Utah, m . J. F. Arrowsmith. X

420 Sarah Elizabeth, b. Feb. 10, 1885, at Linden, Apache County, Ariz., m. F. S. Maddox. X

421 Andrew, b. Oct. 4, 1887, at Linden.

422 Bradford Parley, b. Feb. 1, 1890, at Linden.

423 Merlin, b. July 27, 1892, at Linden.

424 Lettia Maria, b. Nov. 23, 1894, at Linden.

425 Zina, b. Jan. 31, 1897, at Linden.

426 James Melvin, b. July 21, 1903, at Ogden, Utah.

MERLIN J. STONE, SR. 140

MARIA (BAKER) STONE 140

(140)

MERLIN JONES STONE (see 59, Stone lineage, this volume) was born Nov. 26, 1853, at Bountiful, Davis County, Utah. Married Jan. 17, 1878, at Richmond, Cache County, Utah, by Archibald Kerr, Justice of the Peace, Maria, daughter of Simon and Elizabeth (Staples) Baker. She was born Nov. 8, 1860, at Salt Lake City, Utah.

Mr. Stone came with his parents to Ogden, Utah, during the latter part of March, 1857, where he received a common school education, and by study at home and private lessons, he acquired a fair business education. From 1876 to 1882 he worked at farming during the summer months, and taught writing, bookkeeping and shorthand classes during the winter in Weber and Cache Counties. In 1883 he removed to Beaver Canyon, Idaho, where he entered into the general merchandise business. He helped to organize that place into a school district and was its first trustee. He was also Justice of the Peace in 1884-5 and was re-elected to the same position. He returned to Ogden in the fall of 1890, where he has since resided.

Mr. Stone was charter member of Wasatch Council No. 520 of the National Union and was also charter member of the Woodmen of the World, Camp No. 74, of Ogden, in which order he has been a "chopper" since 1896.

He was unanimously elected vice president of the John Stone Association at their annual reunion held at Milford, Conn., Aug. 29, 1894.

Their return to Ogden was principally as the result of Mrs. Stone's determination that her children should not be denied the privilege of securing an education such as the public schools of Ogden offered to them, since there were no further opportunities in the little Idaho town.

Two more children were added to the family at Ogden, the twins, Merlin Jones, Jr., and Mabel Elizabeth; but the little girl only remained with them eight short years, when she was called to the Great Beyond.

Mrs. Stone is a woman of strong character, possessing remarkable fortitude and courage, which has been most beautifully shown in her home to which she has devoted, and is devoting her life. Too much can not be attributed to her for the success of her children, who have responded to the determination and efforts of their mother, by becoming independent citizens, a credit to any community. Her influence has also spread in a quiet way, and many are they who might tell of her helpfulness to them when in doubt and trouble.

She is a member of the Ogden Circle No. 581 of the Women of Woodcraft.

Children:

427 Daisy Louella, b. Dec. 9, 1878, at Ogden, Utah, m. John W. Wintle. X
428 Bertha Maria, b. Aug. 15, 1882, at Ogden, Utah. X
429 Effie Maude, b. May 24, 1887, at Beaver Canyon, Idaho. X
430 Merlin Jones, b. May 2, 1891, at Ogden, Utah. X
431 Mabel Elizabeth, b. May 2, 1891, at Ogden, Utah, d. April 7, 1899, at Ogden, Utah. X

(144)

CHARLES HOEPHI married November, 1896, Alida Baker. She was born Dec. 22, 1856.
Children:
432 Willie, b. July 18, 1878.
433 Rudolph, b. 1880.
434 Winfield S., b. 1883.

(149)

WILLIAM BOYLE married Clarrissa E. Baker. Born Oct. 21, 1849.
Children:
435 Lorin, b. 1867.
436 Emma, b. 1870.
437 Mary, b. 1873.
438 Carrie, b. 1875 (twin).
439 Charley, b. 1875 (twin).
440 Harriet, b. 1878.
441 Edith, b. 1880.
442 Mabel, b. 1884.
443 Estella, b. 1886.

MERCY R. BAKER 160.

(160)

MERCY RACHEL BAKER was born Sept. 29, 1865, at Mendon, Utah. She received her early education at home, in the public schools of Mendon and the schools of Logan.

After graduating from the Brigham Young College at Logan, she took up the profession of teaching. Later she was employed as critic teacher in the Normal Training Department of the Brigham Young College. She occupied her leisure time in study and her vacations were spent in Summer Schools.

The summer of 1895-6 she attended the Utah State University.

The fall of 1896 she went east and resumed her educational work with some of the most eminent doctors and professors.

She entered the Emerson College of Oratory and the Posse gymnasium at Boston, Mass., and later she entered Dr. Sargent's Sanitary gymnasium at Cambridge. She also studied at the Harvard University 1898 and 1899, and in 1901 she graduated with high honors from the Emerson College of Oratory.

She was an instructor of elocution and physical education; also a public reader in Boston and Cambridge. After graduating she spent some time in visiting the leading schools, colleges and universities of the east.

In 1902-3 she took charge of the department of oratory and physical education in the Oneida Stake Academy at Preston, Idaho.

In 1904 she established in Salt Lake a private school, which is known as the Baker School of Oratory and Dramatic Art and School for Stammerers. It is located on the second floor of the Constitution Building, 34 South Main Street.

The school has continued to grow in strength and prominence until now, 1911, the equipment is better, the enrollment is larger and the results of the work is greater than it has been any year since its organization. Miss Baker does a great deal of work outside of her teaching in the form of readings, lectures and recitals.

CARL BAKER NYMAN 444.

MARY A. (BAKER) NYMAN 162

(162)

CARL ANDREW NYMAN of Greenville, Utah, was born Oct. 20, 1871, at Logan, Utah. Married June 20, 1894, at Logan, Utah, Mary Agnes, daughter of Jarvis Y. and Rachel (Richards) Baker. She was born Aug. 29, 1870, at Mendon, Utah.

MRS. NYMAN was a child of extraordinary activity and made many adventures which other children of her age were afraid to undertake.

When only four years old she commenced school and oftentimes would become too tired and sleepy to keep awake; then the teacher would make a bed of the children's wraps and let her take a nap. She had only attended school a short time when her parents moved on to a farm two and one-half miles northwest of Mendon and, of course, she was taken from school.

Living so far from town it was impossible to attend school regularly. She received her education little by little in the Mendon public schools. She owes a great deal of her early training to the efforts of her father and also to her brother Jarvis, who taught her reading, spelling and the rudiments of arithmetic.

She was baptised and confirmed a member of the Church of Jesus Christ of Latter Day Saints by her father, when she was eight years old. Soon after this a very peculiar thing happened. While she was watching the sheep a ram from the flock attacked and butted her until she was almost lifeless. This was followed by a severe illness of three weeks.

In September, 1888, she commenced school at the Brigham Young College, where she attended one year, after which she began teaching. She taught successfully in the Benson Ward one year, Greenville two years, Lewiston one year and Cache Junction, Utah, one year.

On the third of May, 1890, while teaching school at Benson Ward she was struck by lightning, being rendered unconscious and having her clothing literally burned and torn from her body. She received a number of bad burns, the scars of which remain to this day. A few moments after being struck by lightning it started to rain and when she was found an hour later by a farmer and his son, who were working near by, she was drenched, the rain having put out the fire which might have burned her to death. She was carried into a farm house, where everything possible was done for her relief. She remained bedfast a week and when she heard that the board of trustees were going to employ another teacher she arose from her bed and began teaching while her body was fearfully lacerated and a mass of burns. The doctor said that her great effort to get around and return to her school saved her from paralysis.

July 5th, 1898, she left her husband's home and has since then provided for herself and boy, which has been no easy matter. She has been book agent, has boarded college students and nursed the sick in order to earn her living and keep her boy in school.

Recently much of her time has been spent working in the temple for the dead, many of whom have been her deceased ancestors.

Children:
444 Carl Baker, b. June 7, 1895, atGreenville, Utah.

(163)

ELIZABETH ORILLA BAKER, daughter of Jarvis Y. and Rachel (Richards) Baker, was born July 5, 1873, at Mendon, Utah. She was taken ill on May 1st, and after intense suffering with diphtheria and brain fever she died on May 11, 1878.

Although she was scarcely five years old she showed marked mental ability and a beautiful, unselfish disposition. She was loved dearly by her parents, brothers, sisters and all who came in contact with her, and when she passed away, that light and comfort that her soul rendered departed from the home.

LUCY MARIA BAKER 164

(164)

LUCY M. BAKER, daughter of Jarvis Y. and Rachel (Richards) Baker, was born June 21, 1875, at Mendon, Utah, where she attended the public schools until 1893, and 1894 she attended the B. Y. College at Logan, Utah. On May 1, 1895, she took up the study of nursing and obstetrics and Oct. 6, 1896, she received her diploma for obstretrics and nursing from the Utah State Medical Board.

In December, 1896, she went to Morgan, Utah, where she practiced obstetrics and nursing for three years. While at Morgan she was elected city recorder Nov. 6, 1898.

In 1900 she went to Logan, Utah, working at her profession there and throughout the northern part of Utah and southern Idaho.

In 1904 she went to Chicago, Detroit and other cities, where she attended the clinics to help her in her chosen profession, and in July, 1906, she went to Salt Lake City, where she is engaged in nursing. She has been called professionally to Idaho, Wyoming, California, New York and other states, and is one of Utah's best and well-known nurses. Her residence is at 237-8 Constitutional Building, Salt Lake City.

JAMES C. AND LYDIA A. (BAKER) HOGENSEN 166

(166)

JAMES CHRISTIAN HOGENSEN, son of Neils and Bodel (Monson) Hogenson, is a native of Denmark, having been born at Vester Alling, Randers, Jutland, July 24, 1874. He married Dec. 24, 1903, in the Latter Day Saints' Temple, at Logan, Utah, Lydia Aurelia, daughter of Jarvis Y. and Rachel (Richards) Baker. She was born April 6, 1879, at Mendon, Utah.

The Hogenson family came to Logan in 1880, moved to Richmond in 1882 and finally settled at Newton, Cache County, Utah, in 1885.

Mr. Hogenson's elementary schooling was obtained in the early, ungraded schools of Richmond and Newton. He succeeded in completing the eighth grade in the latter town, and entered the U. A. C. for the winter course in 1895. He liked the school so well that he returned and began a course in commerce, from which he was graduated with the degree of B. S. in 1899. He supported himself while getting his college training, by working on the farm, on canals, railroads, etc., during vacations. While in school he was president for one term of the Longfellow Literary Society, which was engaged in debating and literary work. He was first sergeant under Lieutenant Styer, and First Lieutenant under Captain Dunning.

Immediately after graduating, Mr. Hogenson taught at Clarkston, being at the same time county fruit tree inspector for one year. From 1900 to 1902 he was principal of the Newton schools.

In the fall of 1902 he entered Michigan Agricultural College at East Lansing, Mich., where he registered for post-graduate work in horticulture and in soils. On January 1, 1903, he accepted a position with the United States Department of Agriculture in the Bureau of Soils at Washington, D. C. Here he was under the direct supervision of Prof. T. H. King, who that summer established various new stations for soil investigation. During several summers Mr. Hogenson had charge, respectively, of the Government Experiment Station in Southern Maryland, in Lancaster, Pa., and at Anderson, Ind. In the summer of 1905 Mr. Hogenson was given charge of the co-operative work at the Experiment Station, Kingston, R. I., and in October he was transferred to Ithaca, N. Y., there to do co-operative work with the Cornell Experiment Station. About a month later he resigned from the service and entered Cornell to do post-graduate work in agronomy and horticulture with Professors Hunt and Bailey. He received the degree of M. S. A. in June, 1906. This year Mr. Hogensen returned to the West and founded the Department of Agriculture in the Fielding Academy of Paris, Idaho. The next year, 1907, he was given the position of Professor of Agronomy at the Utah Agricultural College at Logan, Utah, as well as Station Agronomist, which positions he still holds.

Mrs. Hogenson was born on a farm about three miles northwest of Mendon, Utah. Living so far out of town, it was difficult to get to school, so the children did considerable studying at home. It was no uncommon thing, in the evening, to see the children seated around the table studying until a late hour. In this way Lydia became a good reader before she began school, being placed in the second reader when she began. The first school she attended was at Mendon when she was eight years old. Here she attended only a few months during each year for four years. She also attended the public schools of Petersboro for a short time and also the public schools of Logan for about four months. In September, 1896, she entered the B. Y. College and began work upon the four year normal course, which she completed in June, 1900. While at the college she was selected by her class during her senior year to dedicate the class tree on Arbor day and she was also the class orator at the class day exercises during commencement.

After leaving college she was engaged to teach the primary school at Newton, Utah. Here she taught for two years. During the school year 1902-3 she taught in the city schools of Logan. While at Newton she did more than teach school because she captured the principal, Mr. J. C. Hogenson.

Soon after they were married they went to Washington, D. C., where Mr. Hogenson was engaged as a soil expert in the United States Department of Agriculture. The summer of 1904 was spent at Anderson, Ind., returning to Washington later and then attending the World's Fair at St. Louis. From here Lydia came home to Utah with her sister Lucy.

In February, 1905, word was received of the death of her brother, Hyrum, who was killed in a railroad wreck at Milton, N. D. When Doloris was three months old Mrs. Hogenson made the journey from Mendon, Utah,, to Washington, D. C., alone to join her husband and soon after arriving they moved to Kingston, R. I., where Mr. Hogenson had been assigned to do co-operative work with the R. I. Experiment Station. Here they spent six months enjoying the ocean breezes of Rhode Island and then moved to Ithaca, N. Y.

While in Ithaca Mrs. Hogenson received word of the death of her brother, Asa, in the mountains west of Mendon, Utah, and immediately left with her little girl for home, arriving in time for the funeral.

They still reside at Logan, where Mrs. Hogenson is an officer and an active worker in the B. Y. College Alumni Association. She is also a member of the Stake Board of the Y. L. M. I. A. of Cache Stake. She is enjoying her work and is striving to the best of her ability to perform the duties which God has placed before her.

Children:
445 Melba Doloris, b. Dec. 20, 1904, at Mendon, Utah.
446 Helen Aurelia, b. May 18, 1908, at Logan, Utah.

FREDERICK CHESTER SORENSEN 447. EMMA T. (BAKER) SORENSEN 167

(157)

FREDERICK JACOB SORENSON, son of Jacob and Susan (Hancock) Sorenson, was born Aug. 12, 1876, at Mendon, Utah. Died there June 25, 1909. Married June 12, 1907, in the Latter Day Saints' Temple at Logan, Utah, Emma Theresa, daughter of Jarvis Y. and Rachel (Richards) Baker. She was born Sept. 7, 1880, at Mendon, Utah.

Emma Theresa's first educational instructions were received under the direction of her parents and older brothers and sisters at home, being nine years of age when first entering the public schools of Mendon, and ranking among the foremost of her classmates of the same age.

After attending the public schools of Mendon and Logan she entered the B. Y. College of Logan, Utah, where she met with much success with her labors. In connection with her college work she took up the study of voice culture.

In September, 1901, she began teaching in the public schools of Mendon and the following two years were spent teaching in the County Schools of Box Elder. In the fall of 1904 she entered the Latter Day Saints' University at Salt Lake City. During this year and those that followed she again took up the study of Voice Culture, Harmony and Composition. She was left a widow two years after her marriage.

Children:
447 Frederic Chester, b. April 8, 1908, at Mendon, Utah.

AGNES MERCY BAKER 175

(175)

AGNES MERCY BAKER, daughter of Amenzo White and Agnes (Steele) Baker, was born June 6, 1870, at Mendon, Utah, and died there March 13, 1888.

HANNAH (BAKER) BUIST 178

(178)

DAVID BUIST, son of David and Agnes (Burnett) Buist, was born Feb. 23, 1872, at Arbroath, Scotland. He married June 5, 1900, at Mendon, Utah, Hannah Maria, daughter of Amenzo White and Agnes (Steel) Baker. She was born Oct. 23, 1876, at Mendon, Utah.
Children:
448 Annie Agnes, b. Sept. 24, 1902, at Border, Bear Lake County, Idaho.
449 Earl Amenzo, b. Dec. 28, 1904, at Border, Bear Lake County, Idaho.

(180)

SAMUEL GEORGE SPENCER, son of Daniel and Mary Jane (Cutliffe) Spencer, was born Feb. 14, 1864, at Salt Lake City, Utah. He married Oct. 14, 1885, in the Latter Day Saints Temple, at Logan, Utah, Jane Maria, daughter of Albert Mowry and Edna Jane (Coon) Baker. She was born May 8, 1867, at Mendon, Utah. They reside at 264 Canyon Road, Salt Lake City, where Mr. Spencer is manager of the Ensign Grocery Co.

Children:

450 Albert Baker, b. Oct. 30, 1888, at Mendon, Utah, d. same day.
451 Alma, b. Aug. 24, 1890, Pleasant Green, Salt Lake County, Utah.
452 David, b. Dec. 1, 1891, at Pleasant Green, Salt Lake County, Utah.
453 Pearl, b. Aug. 27, 1893, at Mendon, Utah.
454 Clawson, b. March 13, 1898, at Pleasant Green, d. Oct. 30, 1898.
455 Rhoda, b. March 23, 1899, at Pleasant Green.
456 Zina, b. Sept. 24, 1900, at Pleasant Green.
457 Owen, b. Sept. 8, 1901, at Pleasant Green, d. February, 1902.
458 Ruth, b. Dec. 17, 1902, at Pleasant Green, d. June 6, 1903.
459 Charles, b. May 26, 1904, at Pleasant Green, d. May 27, 1904.

SARAH E. BAKER 182

(182)

SARAH ELIZABETH BAKER, daughter of Albert M. and Edna Jane (Coon) Baker, was born Feb. 6, 1872, at Mendon, Utah, where her early life was spent attending school and later, taking special advanced studies.

In 1896-7 Miss Baker studied obstetrics at Salt Lake City, under the instruction of Dr. Martha H. Cannon, and was graduated from the obstretrical course July, 1897.

In 1899 she removed to Logan, Utah, where clinical work and study of diseases was taken up under some of the foremost physicians of that city. Since that time she has been one of the leading nurses in Cache County; also devoting much time in various parts of Utah and Idaho. In her profession as nurse, through her labor of patience and love, she has gained a host of friends; in her home town she has done much charity work among the sick, and in her home she has been as a ministering angel to the members of the family circle.

Miss "Sadie" for many years has been a church worker in the Latter Day Saints Church, in her home town, holding positions in Primary, Y. L. M. I. A. and assisting along other lines in church work.

She now, 1911, resides at her old home at Mendon, Utah.

(185)

JAMES PETER JENSEN, son of James Peter and Christina Jensen, was born Oct. 12, 1875, at Newton, Cache County, Utah. Married June 14, 1901, at Logan, Utah, Laura, daughter of Albert Mowry and Edna Jane (Coon) Baker. She was born June 11, 1881, at Mendon, Utah.

Mr. Jensen, while a student at the Brigham Young College at Logan, Utah, enlisted in the United States service in the Spanish-American war and went to Manila, where he acquired the distinction of being a brave soldier.

After returning from Manila, at the close of the war, he first engaged in school teaching and afterwards accepted a position with a hardware firm at Brigham City, Utah. About 1905 he removed to Malad, Idaho, where he entered in the lumber and hardware business, and is now, 1911, continuing in the same line of business at Malad.

Children:
460 Mabel, b. March 4, 1902, at Mendon, Utah.
461 Peter Raymond, b. July 15, 1903, at Brigham City, Utah, d. July 25, 1903.
462 Laura La Rue, b. Aug. 5, 1904, at Brigham City, Utah.
463 Royal Baker, b. Oct. 1, 1906, at Malad City, Idaho.
464 Edna, b. Jan. 26, 1908, at Malad City, Idaho.
464½ Albert Rex, b. Sept. 6, 1910, at Malad City, Idaho.

EDNA BAKER 178

(187)

EDNA BAKER, daughter of Albert M. and Edna Jane (Coon) Baker, was born June 2, 1888, at Mendon, Utah, where she attended the public schools, from which she was graduated May, 1901.

She attended the B. Y. College at Logan, Utah, during 1903 to 1907. Graduated from the Kindergarten Normal course of that institution in May, 1907.

In 1907-8, she taught in the district schools of Francis, Summit County, Utah, and since that time has been a successful teacher in the public schools of her home town.

Miss Edna has been an ardent worker in the Primary Association, and Y. L. M. I. A., and is now, 1911, engaged in Sunday School work in the Latter Day Saints Church.

MARY E. (BAKER) JENSEN 189

(189)

JENS JENSEN, son of Neils and Karen (Forkeldsen) Jensen, was born at Brigham City, Utah; married December 17, 1885, in the Latter Day Saints Temple, at Logan, Utah, Mary Emma, daughter of George W. and Agnes (Richards) Baker. She was born July 30, 1864, at Mendon, Utah. After graduating from the district school at Mendon, she attended the Brigham Young College one year at Logan, Utah, and afterwards taught a district school for four years.

Children: Born in Mendon, Utah.
465 Sibyl, b. Dec. 21, 1886, m. July 28, 1909, in the Latter Day Saints Temple, at Logan, Utah, Clement, son of Thomas and Frances (Vanoy) Smith.
466 Victor, b. Dec. 17, 1888, d. Feb. 11, 1889.
467 Mary, b. Jan. 30, 1890, m. July 28, 1909, in the Latter Day Saints Temple, at Logan, Utah, Atherton, son of Lucien C. and Sarah (Holden) Farr.
468 Agnes, b. Jan. 10, 1892.
469 Lillian, b. June 12, 1894.
470 Esther, b. March 5, 1896.
471 Milton, b. July 19, 1898.
472 Olive, b. Sept. 3, 1902.

JULIA (BAKER) CHRISTENSEN 190

(190)

FRANKLIN ROBESPIERRE CHRISTENSEN, son of Andrew and Marion (Williamson) Christensen, was born July 14, 1864, at Brigham, Utah. He married Aug. 24, 1887, in the Latter Day Saints Temple at Logan, Utah, Julia, daughter of George W. and Agnes (Richards) Baker. She was born Aug. 3, 1866, at Mendon, Utah, where at the age of six years she entered the town school, where she completed the prescribed course, and in 1885 she accepted a position to teach school at Teton, Idaho, and the following year she was employed to teach at Hyrum, Cache County, Utah.

After marriage they resided in Mendon, Utah, where Mr. Christensen was the principal of the school. They moved to North Ogden, where he was engaged in the same profession and the following year, 1889, he accepted the position as instructor in the Ogden High School and remained in the employ of the school board of Ogden for eighteen years. In 1901 Mrs. Christensen again took up the vocation of teaching, being employed in the Ogden schools for four years.

Mr. Christensen also studied law, and while he was admitted to the bar, to practice before the courts of the state, he never adopted the practice as a profession. They removed to Salt Lake City in 1905, where Mrs. Christensen continued to teach for three years and where Mr. Christensen holds a position in one of the railway offices. They reside at 265 West Fifth South Street, Salt Lake City.

Children:
473 Corinne, b. Dec. 21, 1888, at North Ogden, Utah.
474 Franklin, b. Oct. 29, 1890, at Ogden, Utah, died there Jan. 2, 1891.
475 Florence, b. Jan. 10, 1892, at Ogden, Utah, died there Feb. 28, 1892.
476 George, b. Jan. 21. 1895, at Ogden, Utah.

LUCY A. (BAKER) JOHNSON 192

(192)

CHARLES AUGUSTUS JOHNSON, son of George Washington and Miriam Sylvina (Gibson) Johnson, was born.................................. He married April 27, 1891, at Smithfield, Cache County, Utah, Lucy Agnes, daughter of George W. and Agnes (Richards) Baker. She was born June 2, 1871, at Mendon, Utah, where she attended the district school. She took a course and graduated in fancy needle-work She remained at home until marriage.

Children:
477 Juanita Ione, b. July 3, 1892, at Mendon.
478 Gladys Lucile, b. Nov. 2, 1893, at Anaconda, Mont., d. Sept. 4, 1899, at Ogden.
479 Avice Helen, b. Sept. 29, 1895, at Anaconda, Mont.
480 Charles Howard, b. April 2, 1897, at Mendon, Utah.
481 Irma Patricia, b. March 17, 1901, at Ogden, Utah.
482 Joseph Russell, b. Sept. 25, 1904, at Brigham City, Utah.

CELESTIA (BAKER) HOWELL 196

(196)

WILLIAM M. HOWELL, son of Senator Joseph and Mary E. (Maughan) Howell, was born at Wellsville, Cache County, Utah, and married Nov. 12, 1903, in the Latter Day Saints Temple at Logan, Utah, Celestia, daughter of George W. and Agnes (Richards) Baker. She was born September 1, 1881, at Mendon, Utah; graduated at the district school at Mendon. Attended the Agricultural College at Logan two years before her marriage.

Children:

483 William Radcliffe, b. Aug. 2, 1904, d. Feb. 13, 1907, at Logan, Utah.
484 Spencer Baker, b. Sept. 5, 1908, at Logan, Utah.
484½ boy.

OLIVE (BAKER) HATCH 197

(197)

H. SUMNER HATCH, son of Hezekiah Eastman and Georgia (Thatcher) Hatch. Married June 30, 1909, in the Latter Day Saints Temple at Logan, Utah, Olive, daughter of George W. and Agnes (Richards) Baker. She was born July 10, 1885, at Mendon, Utah. She attended the district schools at Mendon, graduating in 1900. The year of 1901-2 was spent at the New Jersey Academy at Logan, Utah. and the two following years at the Brigham Young College, from which institution she graduated in the spring of 1904, and the following fall she began teaching school at Cornish, Idaho, and the next three years she taught in the public schools of Brigham City, Logan and Salt Lake City. They at present are residing at Logan, Utah.

(203)

ALBERT W. RAYBOULD of Salt Lake City, Utah, was born May 23, 1864, at Salt Lake City, Utah. Married September 12, 1887, at Salt Lake City, Utah, Lucy Amelia, daughter of Joseph and Lucy Amelia (Pack) Baker. She was born Oct. 22, 1867, at Mendon, Utah. Mr. Raybould is now, 1910, secretary of the B. P. O. of Elks at Salt Lake City. His parents were William F. and Elizabeth E. Raybould. They were born in England.

Children: Born at Salt Lake City.
485 Douris A., b. Sept. 12, 1888.
486 Lynn W., b. Dec. 25, 1895.

DAVID T. OWENS   CHARLOTTE E. (BAKER) OWENS 204

(204)

DAVID F. OWENS was born September 29, 1862, in Cenkases. Ohio. He married Dec. 14, 1886, at Mendon, Utah, Charlotte Eleanor, daughter of Joseph and Lucy Amelia (Pack) Baker. She was born June 16, 1869, at Mendon, Utah.

Children:
487 Ethel M., b. Jan. 9, 1890, at Mendon, Utah.
488 Alta Tanzon, b. Jan. 21, 1892, at Paragoonah, Utah.
489 Grace Eleanor, b. May 17, 1895, at Paragoonah, Utah, d. Sept. 23, 1895, at Paragoonah.
490 Charlotte, b. July 5, 1900, at Teton, Idaho.
491 Belle, b. Nov. 7, 1907, at Teton, Idaho.

(207)

EDGAR ARLINGTON married in Butte, Mont., Tanzon Louella, daughter of Joseph and Lucy Amelia (Pack) Baker. She was born Feb. 23, 1871, at Mendon, Utah. They separated about 1904 or 1905.

Children:
492 Joseph Baker, b. 1903 at Butte, Mont.

FERRIS E. JONES ALICE (BAKER) JONES 213

(213)

FERRIS E. JONES, son of John J. and Louella (Croft) Jones, was born May 16, 1884, at Logan, Utah. Was married May 3, 1905, by Elder William N. Thomas at Logan, Utah, to Alice M., daughter of Joseph and Mary Alice (Morgan) Baker. She was born March 20, 1884, at Mendon, Utah.

Children:
493 Ferris John, b. March 5, 1906, at Brigham City, Utah.
494 Joseph Lavell, b. Dec. 1, 1907, at Logan, Ptah.

(222)

SAMUEL HENRY SELF, son of Samuel Henry and Margaret Ann (Craven) Self, was born Feb. 24, 1865, at Alexandria, Va. Married Oct. 21, 1896, at Lewiston, Utah, by A. D. Smith, J. P., Charlotte Maria, daughter of Benjamin and Margarette Ann (Rowe) Baker. She was born June 7, 1877, at Lewiston, Utah.

Children: Born at Lewiston.
495 Bertha Margaret, b. Dec. 23, 1897.
496 Henry Irvin, b. June 15, 1900.
497 James Merlin, b. Nov. 29, 1902.
498 Mabel Pearl, b. Jan. 27, 1906.
499 Laura Ann, b. May 23, 1908.

Samuel Henry Self, Sr., was born June 19, 1833, at Washington, D. C., and married at Alexandria, Va., Margaret Ann Craven. She was born 1845 at Alexandria, Va.

(238)

HENRY W. MATKIN, fourth son of Samuel and Sarah Ann (Wilkes) Matkin, was born April 11, 1875, at Hyde Park, Cache County, Utah. Married April 2, 1894, at Cardston, Canada, Mildred, daughter of Samuel L. and Ann Eliza (Leavitt) Baker. She was born July 17, 1877, at Wellsville, Cache County, Utah.

Mr. Matkin's father, Samuel Matkin, was born Aug. 19, 1850, at Lancashire, England, and married in 1869 Sarah Ann Wilkes, who was born November 29, 1853, at St. Louis, Mo. He died Jan. 16, 1905, at Cardston, Alta, Canada.

Children of H. W. and Mildred (Baker) Matkin.
500 William Henry, b. April 24, 1896, at Cardston, Alta, Canada.
501 Bert B., b. Oct. 4, 1898, at Leavitt, Alta, Canada.
502 Lois, b. Oct. 22, 1900, at Leavitt, Alta, Canada.
503 Gladys, b. July 9, 1902, at Leavitt, Alta, Canada.
504 Mildred, b. Jan. 23, 1905, at Leavitt, Alta, Canada.
505 Harold Lynn, b. June 1, 1907, at Leavitt, Alta, Canada.
506 Muriel, b. March 29, 1909, at Leavitt, Alta, Canada.

(239)

JOSEPH McKAY LEISHMAN, son of Robert and Ellen (McKay) Leishman, was born July 7, 1870, at Wellsville, Utah. He married Oct. 1, 1896, at Cardston, Canada, Martha, daughter of Samuel L. and Ann Eliza (Leavitt) Baker. She was born May 5, 1879, at Mendon, Cache County, Utah.

Mr. Leishman's father was born in Scotland and his mother was born in Ireland.

Children: Born at Cardston, Canada.
507 Ellen B., b. July 11, 1897.
508 LeVern, b. May 19, 1899.
509 Le Roy, b. April 22, 1902.
510 Samuel, b. Aug. 30, 1905.
511 Idonna, b. Sept. 3, 1908.

(240)

OLAF ALBERT OLSEN, son of Albert and Elsie (Benson) Olsen, was born Dec. 18, 1876, at Lund, Sweden. He married Dec. 18, 1899, at Leavitt, Alberta, Canada, Charlotte, daughter of Samuel L. and Ann Eliza (Leavitt) Baker. She was born March 21, 1881, at Mendon, Utah.

Children: Born at Leavitt, Canada.
512 Elsie, b. April 28, 1901.
513 Annie, b. Dec. 29, 1902, d. Feb. 18, 1903.
514 Oliver, b. Dec. 21, 1904.
515 Keneth Albert, b. Jan. 21, 1907.
516 Samuel Aaron, b. April 18, 1909, d. Dec. 20, 1909.

(241)

SIMPSON ARTHUR MATKIN, son of Samuel and Sarah Ann (Wilkes) Matkin, was born March 1, 1877, at Hyde Park, Cache County, Utah, married April 29, 1902, at Leavitt, Canada, Annie L., daughter of Samuel L. and Ann Eliza (Leavitt) Baker. She was born Aug. 23, 1883, at Mendon, Utah.
517 Elmer B., b. Sept. 8, 1903, at Leavitt, Canada.
518 Vivian B., b. April 4, 1905, at Magrath, Canada.
519 Lottie Madeline, b. Jan. 30, 1908, at Magrath, Canada.
520 Hazel, b. Nov. 5, 1909.

(242)

JAMES LAWRENCE LYNDS, son of John Edmund and Ida May (McNult) Lynds, was born Sept. 31, 1881, at North River, Coalchester County, Nova Scotia. He married June 30, 1910, at Leavitt, Canada, Alta Esther, daughter of Samuel L. and Ann Eliza (Jenkins) Baker. She was born Nov. 28, 1886, at Mendon, Utah.

Note—John Edmund Lynds was born at Boston, Mass. Married March 27, 1879, Ida May McNult. She was born at North River, Nova Scotia.

LAURA LOUISA BAKER 254

(254)

LAURA LOUISA BAKER, daughter of James S. and Louisa (Staples) Baker, was born Aug. 5, 1880, at Franklin, Cache County, Utah, and died June 23, 1884, at Ogden, Utah. She is buried in the Ogden City cemetery.

RUTH BAKER 259.

(259)

RUTH BAKER, daughter of James S. and Elizabeth (Cunningham) Baker, was born Jan. 17, 1892, at Beckwith, Wyo.

She was graduated from the grammar school at Acton, Cal., 1906, and in 1910 was graduated with honors from the Brownsberger Home School at Los Angeles, Cal.

She mastered the course in stenography and upon her graduation accepted a position as stenographer and typist and is now 1911 filling a responsible position with one of the leading law firms at Los Angeles, Cal.

BLANCHE BAKER 261

(261)

BLANCH BAKER, daughter of James S. and Elizabeth (Cunningham) Baker, was born September 21, 1895, at Lovelocks, Nev. She now resides with her parents at Keene, Cal., where she will complete her course at the common schools this spring and will be ready to enter the higher grades in September, 1911.

NINA BELLE BAKER 263

(263)

NINA BELLE BAKER, daughter of Henry and Isabell (Dennett) Baker, was born May 5, 1903, at Mesa, Ariz., where she now (1911) resides with her father.

RENA RACHEL BAKER 264   NINA BAKER 265

(264)

RENA RACHEL BAER, daughter of Jarvis A. and Pauline (Pefferle) Baker, was born December 4, 1891, at Baker City, Oregon, and is now (1911) residing in Salt Lake City.

(265)

NINA BAKER, daughter of Jarvis A. and Pauline (Pefferle) Baker, was born July 20, 1893, at Ellensburg, Wash.

(314)

CYRUS HARRINGTON came to Leydon, Mass., where he married Sally Avery.

Children:
521 Sidney married Desire, daughter of Thomas J. Shepardson.

(325)

JERRAH C. MINER was born April 28, 1835, at Leydon, Mass.; died June 3, 1894, at Northfield, Mass.; married Caroline L. Brown; she was born Jan. 2, 1840, at Whitingham, Vt. She now (1910) is residing with her daughter, Genevra Hastings, at Haines City, Fla.

Children:
522 M. Genevra, b. Sept. 19, 1861, Leydon, Mass., m. Wm. Hastings. X.
523 Leon J., b. Dec. 19, d. May 12, 1865, at Colaraine, Mass.
524 Angie L., b. Oct. 29, 1872, Leydon, Mass., d. Jan. 13, 1892, Guilford, Vt.
525 Alton J., b. March 7, 1875, Leydon, Mass.
526 Arlou R., b. April 28, 1881, Guilford, Vt.

WILLIAM H. SHEPARDSON, JR. 328

(328)

WILLIAM HENRY SHEPARDSON, JR., son of William H. and Mary (Baker) Shepardson, was born Dec. 2, 1823, at Coleraiu, Mass., and died in 1904 at Glenwood, Iowa.

Mr Shepardson was a bachelor. He came with his parents in the spring of 1846 to Nauvoo, Ill., and later to Mills County, Iowa. He possessed a fair education and wrote a beautiful hand. He ably assisted the author of this work in his researches, furnishing him with many records and incidents of family history for the same.

He resided at Glenwood, Iowa, where he became an extensive farmer; his two miaden sisters, Lucinda and Salome living with him.

He was in the war of the Rebellion. His war record as written by himself Jan. 12, 1889, to his cousin, Amenzo W. Baker, follows:

Enlisted the tenth day of October, 1861, for three years unless sooner discharged. After the company was filled up to 103 officers and men it was ordered to report at Davenport, but after two days' travel our course was changed by orders to report at Keokuk, where we arrived in the first half of November, and were mustered into the United States service the 17th day of November, 1861.

Our company being the sixth company mustered, was Company F., and regiment was the 15th Iowa Infantry. Another company was mustered a day or two after, but it took a good while to fill up companies H, I and K. However, we were ready and waiting before the ice went out so they could get a boat up to take us to Benton Barracks, where we stayed a week or two and drew arms, accoutrements, wagons, ambulances, tools, etc.

We left St. Louis the first day of April for the Tennessee River and reached Pittsburg, landing the morning of the 6th, just as the battle of Shiloh commenced. Had been ordered to report to Gen. Prentiss, but before the colonel could reach Gen. Prentiss' headquarters he was ordered to take the regiment to another part of the field.

When the regiment left Keokuk there were 1,046 officers and men belonging to it, some of whom were left at Keokuk sick, others left sick at Benton Barracks and some were sick on the boat when we reached Pittsburg, so what with the guard left on the boat there were 760 men went into battle, formed line of battle facing nearly south half a mile north of Shiloh Church and advanced south.

Our fighting was done near the middle of the day, between one-half and one-fourth of a mile north of Shiloh Church, where we lost 189 men in a couple of hours. Later in the day we were in support of batteries nearer the landing, but lost no men there.

At the time of the battle we were not yet assigned to any brigade, but in three or four days were brigaded temporarily with the Sixteenth Iowa and Eighteenth Wisconsin and the latter part of April the Eleventh, Thirteenth, Fifteenth and Sixteenth Iowa regiments were formed into the third brigade of the sixth division, which brigade formation continued till the regiments were all mustered out the last of July, 1865.

The number of the division was afterward changed to the fourth division and we were put in the Seventeenth Army Corps at its formation, so my proper designation was: Company F, Fifteenth Iowa Infantry, third brigade, fourth division, Seventeenth Army Corps, and we always belonged to the "Army of the Tennessee."

I enlisted as a musician. My brother Joseph and J. M. Parsons, who married my sister, Mary, enlisted at the same time and in the same company. My brother had not sufficient endurance and was mustered out the last of July, 1862, for disability. Parsons served his full three years. They were both Sergeants.

The regiment was not engaged the second day in the battle of Shiloh. Afterwards in the advance on Corinth we were under Gen. Thomas, who commanded the right wing, were in the reserve, generally the extreme left of the right wing, were at the front in line of battle whenever it was thought advancing our line might bring on a battle, though we did no actual fighting. After the enemy evacuated Corinth we were about there doing picket duty for awhile and then provost guard in the town till the last of July, when we were sent to Boliver, where we stayed till the enemy had taken Iuka, when we were recalled and sent with the army that went from Corinth to attack the enemy in Iuka. After the enemy were driven out the regiment were provost guard there for ten days and returned to Corinth in time to take part in the battle there the 3rd and 4th day of October, where they lost 109 men. Cannot state the number engaged, but the regiment was pretty well reduced. After the battle, pursued the enemy 50 miles to Ripley, captured batteries and trains, the enemy were compelled to drop, but could not bring them to an engagement, so returned to Corinth.

Left Corinth the forepart of November for Grand Junction, went in camp four miles south of there on the head of Wolf River. While here had division drill (the first we had ever had), and battalion drill on alternate days while preparations were being made for a campaign into Mississippi toward Vicksburg. Started south the last of November down the Mississippi Central railroad; the enemy having burned the railroad bridge across the Tallahatchie River, our brigade was detailed to guard the working party rebuilding it, which took two weeks, then went on overtaking the army in two days.

The day we came up with the rest, the enemy's Cavalry dashed into Holly Springs in the rear of the bridge we had been building, and where our stores had been accumulating and burned the supplies and a great part of the town. So there was nothing but to give up the expedition and go back. The brigade came from Yockena to Holly Springs in two days, four pretty good days march; went from there in a few days to Lafayette on the Memphis & Charleston railroad and after a couple of weeks to Memphis and down the Mississippi River to Duetport, but came back in a week or two to Lake Providence, where the troops composing the Seventeenth Army Corps (which had just been formed) were being got together.

In April went below again and started with the army, going below to cross the Mississippi River, but the brigade was left to guard the route from Millikens' Bend to Perkins' plantation, 43 miles.

After the army had all passed and the river had fallen so as to give us a much shorter land route we went on to New Carthage and Hardtimes Landing and across the Mississippi River to Grand Gulf, where we were ordered to remain and hold the place, so the army in case of disaster would have a safe place to fall back on.

After the army had come around and invested Vicksburg we were ordered up the river and at first were on the extreme left (our proper place would have been the center), but there had been no place left for us there. We were soon sent up the country between the Big Black and Yazoo Rivers with Blair's division to see what force the enemy had in that direction, but found they had not much, and when we returned the town was so completely invested there was no place for us anywhere in the front line, so we camped in rear of our proper place in the line and made details of sharpshooters and men to dig breastworks and build batteries when the lines were advanced.

About ten days before the surrender we were sent with a good many other troops over on to Black River to watch for the army under Gen. Johnston, who was expected to come in from that direction to relieve Vicksburg. There were troops all along the river from Big Black railroad bridge up to Birdsongs Ferry, but Gen. Johnston did not come to time, but we were some 20 miles away when the city surrendered on the 4th of July, 1863. As soon as we had any force in the city a great part of the army started after Gen. Johnston, who fell back into Jackson.

One of our regiments went to bring the train back, we remaining in camp, and when the train was coming in we crossed the river and went across Baker's Creek, where we lay till the train came back loaded. At night orders came to look sharp for that train for a division of the enemy's cavalry had gone up Pearl River on the other side and crossed a good ways up the west side again, so they suspected they meant to strike the train. The Fifteenth had the advance and when we fell in to start in the morning, word came in from the pickets on both the Jackson and Raymond roads that the enemy was in front of them, so we formed in line and waited, but no enemy came, so after a little while we started on. It seems the enemy made captures of a few men between us and Jackson and had learned about the time they struck our pickets that there was a brigade with the train so they gave up trying to capture it and retired.

They had learned before starting that the train had gone back escorted by a single regiment and expected it to return in the same way. It was several miles long when closed up. I pitied the flankers that day, a line on each side of the road; they took intervals like a thin skirmish line, and were instructed to preserve their intervals as well as possible and to keep as nigh 40 rods away from the road as the nature of the ground would admit of and the country is a good deal timbered and full of undergrowth and blackberry briars and the day a hot one in July. We took that train before night into Clinton, a good day's march. Here another brigade took the train and it went through that night without stopping between Champions Hill and Jackson. The mules had neither feed nor water from early morning till nearly the next morning, so you see war is hard not alone on men.

We went no farther than Clinton and after Jackson was evacuated went back towards Vicksburg by easy marches, stopping for a few days at Big Black railroad bridge and then to the city and went into camp the last of July, three or four miles north of town. In August went on an expedition to Monroe, La., some 75 miles back from the river, left the Mississippi at Goodriches Landing, went through a country nearly all heavily timbered, but a great scarcity of water, one stretch 24 miles between drinking places. Only stayed at Monroe a day or two and before we got back to the river more men were sick with chills and fever than the teams could hall, but for a wonder I did not get sick on that campaign which was in some respects the worst I ever saw.

Along in October we moved camp to near the same distance south of the city where eight companies did picket duty till the first of February, the other two companies doing duty as arsenal guard close to town.

In December, 1863, great efforts were made to induce those who had been in the service two years to re-enlist. There were only 472 men left in the regiment, 354 of whom were reported as having re-enlisted. This being three-fourths they were entitled to go home to Iowa in a body and have a furlough of 30 days in the state. Those of the brigade who did not re-enlist were temporarily organized into a battalion under the command of the Major of the 15th Iowa. I did not re-enlist and was always glad I did not for three years was all I could endure and I would likely have died on the Carolina campaign if I had undertaken it. The first of Febraruy, 1854, we started on the Meridian expedition, Gen. Sherman with the 16th and 17th corps. There was little fighting but some hard marching. We lost a few men captured, being a foraging party, were provost guard of Canton nearly a week as we were returning. Destroyed a great deal of railroad and captured a good many mules.

After we came back in March the re-enlisted men went home on their veteran furlough. Some of them were married while at home. I think the furlough was beneficial, for some of the greatest scalawags were as good as the best after it. We stayed in Vicksburg for a while when they were gone, then came up to Mound City, Ill., after a few days up the Tennessee river for the second time as far as Clifton then across the country through Waynesbury, Lawrenceburg, Pulaska, and Athens, Ala., to Huntsville, where we stopped till the regiment overtook us in May. Then by way of Decatur where we crossed the Tennessee river, Gunters Landing, Gaylesville, Rome, Kingston, Etowah and Alltoona Pass, where we left a garrison, to Acworth, where we joined the main army, which starting before us, came another route.

The whole army under Gen. Sherman was composed of the army of the Tennessee under Gen. McPherson consisting of the 15th corps; Gen. Logan, left wing of the 16th corps under Gen. Dodge and 17th corps under Gen. Blair; the Army of the Cumberland under Gen. Thomas consisting of the 14th corps, Gen. Palmer; the 20th corps, Gen. Hooker, and the 4th corps, Gen. Howard. The Army of the Ohio under Gen. Schofield was the 23rd corps.

From the 10th of June to the 5th of September the 15th Iowa was under constant fire, eighty-one days, towit: June 10th to 30th inclusive, 20 days; July 1st to 16th inclusive, 16 days; 20th to

26th inclusive, seven days; 27th to 31st inclusive, five days; August 1st to 26th inclusive, 26 days; 29th to 30th inclusive, two days; September 1st to 5th inclusive, five days.

Days of battle or advance on the enemy or of repulsing attacks, June 15, 19, 23 and 27, four days; July 3, 4, 5, 20, 21, 22 and 28, seven days; August 17, 20, 28 and 31, four days; September 1 and 2, two days—17 days.

The above to my own personal knowledge is substantially true. We lost during this campaign 291 men, but I cannot tell how few there was left at the close. We were 20 miles south of Atlanta when the Twentieth Corps went into the place, but came back there in a few days and rested for a while. On the first day of October started down the Montgomery railroad to see if Hood's army had gone across the Chatahooche River. Went as far as Fairbairn and found they were all across, came back the 3rd and started the 4th after the enemy who were tearing up the railroad in our rear. Went after them through Big Shanty, Allatoona Pass, Kingston, Calhoun to Resaca, where they left the railroad.

Pursued them through Snake Creek Gap, Ships Gap, Lafayette Alpine, Somerville to Gaylesville, where we stopped a couple of weeks when we crossed the Coosa River and started for Marietta by way of Cave Spring, Dallas and New Hope Church. While at Marietta, held presidential election. Left the 13th day of October for Atlanta and started on the morning of the 15th on the march to the sea from Atlanta.

At this time the original members of Company F., who had not re-enlisted, had only two more days to serve. However, as the railroad back was torn up and Atlanta destroyed, there was nothing for it but to go on, so we were mustered out a month after, ten miles southwest of Savannah, Ga., on the Kings Bridge road and came home by way of Fort McAllister, Hilton Head, New York City, Buffalo, Cleveland, Chicago and Davenport, Iowa, where we were paid off, arriving home the 7th day of January, 1865, three years and three months less three days from the time of enlistment, not sick, but pretty well worn out; could not have endured another campaign at that time. Was not wounded, but was hit by a spent ball when on march to the sea, not to cut my clothing, to hurt about as much as a stone thrown by hand.

I was sick several times, about as one is when down with a bad cold, but never to be sent away from the regiment or even sent to the regiment hospital. On the Atlanta campaign I took the regular chills and fever and, though we always broke it up right away, it would return if I overdid or got wet, and I never got rid of it entirely till long after I came home."

"I do not draw a pension, do not know of any just ground on which I could apply for one, yet I think half of those who are pensioned are no more entitled to a pension legally or morally than I am. My brother has a pension of two dollars a month and there is no reason in the world why if he has a pension at all it should not be three or four times as much.

"I think that all the men that I knew in the army had a right feeling toward those opposed; think they had no personal resentment against individuals; would rather capture anyone than to kill him and felt sufficiently kindly toward prisoners always.

" Buren R. Sherman, who was three times elected Governor of Iowa, was a captain in our brigade. I think the Fifteenth Iowa Infantry was in every way as good a regiment and did as much and as good service as any regiment from any state whatever.

"There were 1,908 men in the regiment from first to last, but only 1,763 of them were mustered into the United States service. The casualties of all kinds during the term of service was 1,478. Killed or died of wounds, 139; died of disease, 228; drowned, 4; died in the service, 371; wounded, 466; captured 133; discharged for disability, 257; for wounds, 94.

"We have a brigade reunion every two years. At our last reunion in September, 1887, there were 2,165 of the men of the brigade still living, 711 of whom had belonged to the Fifteenth regiment."

(329)

JONAH M. PARSONS who was born in England, married March, 1853, Mary Shepardson. She was born August 20, 1826, in Colaraine, Mass. He died Nov. 2, 1876, at Percival, Tremont County, Iowa.

Children: Reside at Percival.
527 Alice.
528 Elmer Yetman.
529 Clara.
   2 others d. y.

(330)

JOSEPH SHEPARDSON was born July 25, 1828, at Leydon, Mass., married Feb., 1857, Jane Felch, a widow with three little girls, the oldest 12 years old. Residence, Grand Island Nebr.

Children:
530 Sophia, twin, b. March 31, 1859. d. y.
531 Maria, twin, b. March 31, 1859, m. James C. Kenedy. One son, Roy.

(333)

JAMES LAMBERT married June 7, 1855, Elizabeth Shepardson. She was born March 12, 1837, at Leydon, Mass., d. Dec. 21, 1885, near Norwich, Huron County, Ohio.

Children: All born at Lyons, Mills County, Iowa.
532 Asabel, b. Jan. 19, 1857, m. Missouri Hubbell.
533 Lester Ward, b. Dec. 12, 1858, m. March, 1886, Emma Hubbell.

534 Mary Elizabeth, b. Jan. 11, 1861, m. Jan., 1884, John Merritt. X.
535 Celia Maria, b. March 18, 1864.
536 Calvin, b. Sept. 14, 1866.
537 Wm. Henry, b. Sept. 8. 1868.
538 Janette, b. April 9, 1870.
539 Lewis.
540 Walter.
541 Elsie.

(347)

FRANCIS LEWIS WHITING was born Sept. 22, 1830, married Ann Janette Burdick. She was born Feb. 18, 1831. They belong to the Reorganized Church of Latter Day Saints. He had a brother, Edwin, who settled near, Manti, Utah.
Children.
542 Emma Leone, b. March 8, 1853.
543 Lucia Lovisa, b. March 23, 1855.
544 Ella Janette, b. Dec. 6, 1857.
545 Arthur Wellington, b. Feb. 29, 1860.
546 Mary Bell, b. Jan. 17, 1864.
547 Silvia Cordelia, b. Dec. 10, 1869.
548 Francis Lester, b. Sept. 29, 1874.

All were living in 1892 and all were married, except the youngest, and at that date they had 22 grand children living and four deceased.

SARAH (MINER) BROWN 352

(352)

MINER BROWN, married Sarah Miner. Resides at Thayere, Ia. Mrs. Brown died March 8, 1901, at Thayere.
Children:
549 Fannie M., m. fall of 1896, Wm. Olsinger. Res., 603 Jason St., Denver, Colo.
550 F. Leone, married and lives at Thayere.

(354)

JEFFIE LOOMIS was born 1847 at Clay, N. Y., where he married first, Josie Hoyt, and second, Ella P. Lynn. (No children by second wife.)

Children by first wife:
551 Hoyt, b. 1877.

(356)

CARLOS WEBSTER married Emily C. Smith. She was born Oct. 21, 1839.
Children.
552 Mollie, b. 1869.
553 Frank, b. 1873.

(360)

WILLIE SMITH, married.
Children:
554 Fred and two other children.

(361)

C. EUGENE RATHBUN, born Dec. 12, 1849. Married Anna ———.

Children:
555 Charles Edwin, b. Oct. 25, 1890.

(363)

FRANK A. RATHBUN was born Aug. 28, 1854. Married Susie ———.

Children:
556 Laura, b. Jan. 20, 1877.
557 Harry V., b. Nov. 10, 1886.

(367)

JAMES BUTLER, son of John Lowe and Caroline Farozine (Skeen) Butler, was Born Feb. 18, 1847, at Ponca, on the running water of the Missouri River. He married March 2, 1874, Charlotte Elizabeth, daughter of John and Betsie (Baker) Topham; she was born Dec. 24, 1852, at Parawan, Utah, and died Aug. 24, 1900.

Children:
558 Charlotte Elizabeth, b. Jan. 27, 1875, at Paragoonah, Utah.
559 James Albert, b. June 23, 1876, at Panguitch, Utah.
560 John Topham, b. March 3, 1879, at Panguitch, Utah.
561 Betsie Jane, b. Feb. 9, 1881, at Panquitch, Utah.
562 Caroline Malinda, b. Nov. 14, 1883, at Richfield, Utah.
563 Ernest Horsley, b. Oct. 27, 1885, at Richfield, Utah.

(368)

BISHOP ERNEST SAMUEL HORSELEY, of Price, Carbon County, Utah, son of Samuel Pecket and Sarah (Barrows) Horseley, was born June 16, 1861, at Tottenham, Middlesex, England; married June 5, 1884, in the Latter Day Saints Temple, at St. George, Utah, Mercy Jane, daughter of John and Betsie (Baker) Topham. She was born July 10, 1854, at Parawan, Utah. She died Jan. 19, 1900, at Price, Utah, after many years suffering and her body was brought to her former home at Paragoonah for burial, according to her wishes. The services were conducted by Bishop S. S. Barton. The speakers were R. A. Robinson, John Eyre, Daniel Stone, Bishop Chas. Adams, of Parawan, and Bishop Barton. Having known her from youth up, all eulogized her many good qualities, and offered words of comfort to the bereaved. The remains were escorted by 20 vehicles to the cemetery at Parawan, where her body was intered in the family burying ground.

(369)

JOHN BAKER TOPHAM was born Jan. 23, 1856, at Paragoonah, Iron County, Utah. Married April 19, 1877, in the Latter Day Saints Temple, at St. George, Utah, Mary Jane, daughter of Stephen and Jane Evans (Barton) Smith. She was born March 10, 1860, at Paragoonah.

Children: Born at Paragoonah.
564 John, b. Jan. 6, 1880.
565 Stephen, b. Aug. 23, 1882.
566 Jesse William, b. Dec. 3, 1885.
567 Clara Elva, b. June 27, 1890.
568 Asa Eugene, b. Feb. 13, 1894.

(370)

SIMON THORNTON TOPHAM was born Sept. 21, 1857, at Paragoonah, Utah. Married first Feb. 7, 1878, in the Latter Day Saints Temple, at St. George, Utah, Alice, daughter of John Rolenson and Jane (Coop) Robinson. She was born April 3, 1859, at Paragoonah, Utah.

He married second, June 12, 1884, in the Latter Day Saints Temple, at St. George, Utah, Lucinda Robinson, sister of his first wife. She was born ——.

Children: Born at Paragoonah.
569 Alice Elizabeth, b. Dec. 7, 1878, d. Jan. 30, 1899.
570 Betsie Jane, b. Dec. 12, 1880.
571 Simon Thornton, b. July 29, 1882.
572 Mercy Josephine, b. Oct. 19, 1884.
573 John Coleman, b. Jan. 23, 1889.
574 Joseph Leonard, b. Dec. 1, 1891.
575 Margaret Ellen, b. Nov. 27, 1894.
576 Ina Lauretta, b. Feb. 23, 1904.

Children: By second wife.
577 Mary Jane, b. Sept. 14, 1885.

(371)

THOMAS AMENZO TOPHAM was born Sept. 28, 1859, at Paragoonah, Utah. Married Feb. 17, 1887, in the Latter Day Saints Temple, at St. George, Utah, Annie Maria, daughter of Wilson and Ellen (Nielson) Lund. She was born Oct. 21, 1862, at West Jordon, Salt Lake County, Utah.
Children: Born at Paragoonah.
578 Thomas Amenzo, b. Dec. 18, 1888.
579 Bertha Ellen, b. April 11, 1890.
580 John Karl, b. Nov. 6, 1893.
581 Annie Eliza,, b. March 26, 1896, d. March 28, 1896.

(372)

GEORGE ALBERT TOPHAM was born May 28, 1863, at Paragoonah, Utah, and married Laura, daughter of Samuel Pecket and Sarah (Barrows) Horseley. She was born April 15, 1866, at Plumstead, Kent, England.
Children: Born at Paragoonah, Utah.
582 George Albert, b. Nov. 27, 1891.
583 Laura Alda, b. Dec. 10, 1893.
584 Joseph Ernest, b. Sept. 4, 1895.
585 Sarah Lydia, b. Jan. 3. 1899.
586 Angus Reed, b. Mar. 5. 1905.

(373)

THOMAS ROBINSON, son of John Roleson and Jane (Coop) Robinson, was born Sept. 19, 1863, at Paragoonah, Utah. Married April 30, 1885, in the Latter Day Saints Temple, at St. George, Utah, Susanna Adams, daughter of John and Betsie (Baker) Topham. She was born Sept. 28, 1865, at Paragoonah, Utah.
Children: Born at Paragoonah.
587 Thomas Albert, b. July 4, 1886.
588 Susan Myrtle, b. Dec. 20, 1890.
589 John Orson, b. April 27, 1893, d. Dec. 2, 1893.

(375)

JOSEPH RILEY TOPHAM was born March 1, 1870, at Paragoonah, Utah. Married March 18, 1903, in the Latter Day Saints Temple, at St. George, Utah, Harriet Isabelle, daughter of Josiah and Elizabeth Ann (Norton) Reynolds. She was born July 9, 1877, at Panguitch, Garfield County, Utah.
Children: Born at Paragoonah.
590 Joseph Riley, b. Jan. 8, 1904.
591 Harriet Isabelle, b. May 12, 1905.

(377)

SILAS SANFORD TOPHAM was born April 15, 1874, at Paragoonah, Utah. Married July 17, 1895, in the Latter Day Saints Tem-

ple at Manti, Utah, Amelia, daughter of Peter M. and Mary (Mortenson) Jensen. She was born July 29, 1872, at Parawan, Iron County, Utah. Mr. Topham died July 22, 1905, at Paragoonah, Utah.
Children:
592 Eulala Wrenlock, b. Sept. 8, 1896, at Parawan, Utah.
593 Merlen June, b. May 11, 1900, at Paragoonah.
594 Silas Mardell, twin, b. April 30, 1902, at Paragoonah.
595 Sanford Marlow, twin, b. April 30, 1902, at Paragoonah.
596 Rulon Jensen, b. May 27, 1904.

(379)

THOMAS IRVIN JOHNSON was born Aug. 9, 1865, at St. Charles, Idaho; married Oct. 31, 1886, at Ashley, Uintah County, Utah, Ida, daughter of Taylor and Alice (Stokes) Bird; she was born June 14, 1870.
Children:
597 Thomas Irvin, b. Dec. 4, 1887, Lone Tree, Wyo.
598 Ida May, b. April 29, 1889, Dry Fork, Wyo., m. Robert Harvey. X.
599 Orel Marion, b. May 17, 1891, Dry Fork, Wyo., m. George Graham. X.
600 Rebecca Leonora, b. Aug. 6, 1893, Robertson, Wyo.
601 Alice Isabelle, b. July 15, 1895, Robertson, Wyo.
602 Minnie, b. Oct. 17, 1897, Robertson, Wyo.
603 Maggie, b. June 3, 1900, Robertson, Wyo.
604 Snellen Marion, b. Oct. 15, 1902, Robertson, Wyo.
605 Taylor Reeves, b. Oct. 27, 1904, Robertson, Wyo.
606 Cora Delorus, b. Nov. 25, 1906, Mountain View, Wyo.
607 Norman Deville, b. July 12, 1909, Robertson, Wyo.

(380)

Rev. WILLIAM WALLACE JOHNSON was born Feb. 5, 1867, at St. Charles, Idaho. He mraried Nov. 25, 1901, Alice M., daughter of Henry and Nellie (Scales) Townsend; she was born Nov. 16, 1880. They reside at Robertson, Wyo.
Children:
608 Orville Wallace, b. Sept. 5, 1903, Robertson, Wyo.
609 Lorna Alice, b. May 10, 1905, Robertson, Wyo.
610 Keith Townsend, b. June 12, 1906, Duckville, Uinta County, Wyo.
611 Murl Ielene, b. June 22, 1908, at Silver City, Idaho.

(381)

ALBERT MARIUS JOHNSON was born March 10, 1869, at Lake Town, Rich County, Utah. He married Dec, 9, 1888, at Ashley, Uintah County, Utah, Alice, daughter of Taylor and Alice (Stokes) Bird; she was born Dec. 17, 1867. They reside at Vermal, Utah.
Children:
612 Alice Madeline, b. April 21, 1893, at Lone Tree, Uinta County, Wyo.

JOSEPH A. JOHNSON 382.
SARAH MARGARET (BAKER) JOHNSON 176 and 382

(382)

JOSEPH AMENZO JOHNSON was born Aug. 18, 1871, at Mendon, Utah. Married June 9, 1902, at Paris, Idaho, Sarah Margarette, daughter of Amenzo and Agnes (Steel) Baker; she was born Aug. 19, 1872, at Mendon, Utah.

Children:
613 Dorrit Agnes, b. Jan. 27, 1905, Spring Valley, Wyo.
614 Zelda May, b. April 16, 1906, at Mendon, Utah.
615 Fern Annie, b. Sept. 4, 1907, Robertson, Wyo.
616 Kenneth Baker, b. March 1, 1910, Robertson, Wyo.

DAUGHTERS OF JOSEPH AND MARGARET (BAKER) JOHNSON.
Dorrit Agnes 613.   Fern Annie 615.   Zelva May 614.

(383)

SOLOMON M. HAWKINS, son of Michael and Elizabeth (McNulty) Hawkins, was born Jan. 8, 1869, at New London, Henry County, Iowa. He married April 23, 1902, at Robertson, Uinta County, Wyo., Cora M., daughter of Snellon M. and Rebecca (Baker) Johnson. She was born May 23, 1875, at Lake Town, Rich County, Utah.

Children:
617 Gladys Rebecca, b. Feb. 4, 1904, at Robertson, Wyo.
618 Glenn Michael, b. Aug. 27, 1905, at Robertson, Wyo.

CLAUDE L. JOHNSON 385
CHARLOTTE A. (BAKER) JOHNSON 179 and 385.

(385)

CLAUDE L. JOHNSON was born Feb. 19, 1879, at Rock Springs, Sweet Water County, Wyo. He married Nov. 9, 1908, at Pocatello, Ida., Charlotte Annie, daughter of Amenzo White and Agnes (Steele) Baker; she was born March 22, 1880, at Mendon, Cache County, Utah. They reside at Robertson, Wyo.

Children:
619 Audra, b. Aug. 25, 1910, at Robertson, Wyo.

(389)

CHARLES CLARK was born.................... and married at Sacramento, Cal.,....................Grace, daughter of William C. and Sarah (Baker) Farnsworth. She was born ....at Sacramento.

Children: Born at Sacramento.
620 Albert, b. 1902.
621 Grace, b. 1903.

(394)

THOMAS W. MATHEWS was born April 8, 1866, at Salt Lake City, Utah. He married Sept. 25, 1886, at Salt Lake City, Utah, Annie Gray. She was born———.

Children: All born at Salt Lake City, Utah.
622 Frank W., b. Sept. 3, 1887.
623 Maud, b. Sept. 5, 1889.
624 Thomas, b. May 28, 1891.
625 Lester, b. June, 1894.

(395)

MILES R. TAYLOR married June 29, 1891, at Salt Lake City, Charlotte Ann, daughter of Thomas and Abigail L. (Baker) Mathews. She was born Jan. 5, 1868, in Salt Lake City, and died there, Aug., 1905.

Children: Born at Salt Lake City, Utah.
626 Maud, b. April 18, 1892.
627 Miles, b. Feb. 8, 1898.

(696)

FRANCIS MARION MATHEWS was born Dec. 10, 1869, at Salt Lake City, Utah, where he married, August 8, 1891, Sarah Williams.

Children: Born at Salt Lake City, Utah.
628 Elsie, b. June 15, 1894.
629 Sarah, b. June, 1896.
630 Littie Leah, b. Dec. 24, 1897.
631 Frank, b. July, 1908.

(398)

JOSEPH SIMON MATHEWS was born Dec. 11, 1873, at Salt Lake City, Utah. Married there Jan. 9, 1895, Bessie Ence. She was born ———. He died at Salt Lake City, Utah, Oct. 10, 1905.

Children: Born at Salt Lake City, Utah.
632 Carlton, b. Oct. 23, 1895.
633 Earl b. April 7, 1897.

(399)

ROY BAKER MATHEWS was born Nov. 25, 1875, at Salt Lake City, Utah, where he married, Jan. 29, 1897, Elizabeth Lawrence. She was born——.

Children:
634 Abbie, b. May 30, 1898.
635 Bessie, b. Oct. 9, 1899.
636 Vera, b. Sept. 28, 1907.

(400)

PETER LARSON of Mendon, Utah, son of Magnus and Mary (Anderson) Larson, born ——. Married Sept. 1, 1892, in Mendon, Utah, Charlotte, daughter of William and Charlotte (Baker) Longstroth. She was born Nov. 12, 1868, at Mendon, Utah.

Children: Born at Mendon.
637 Mary, b. March 29, 1893.
638 Vera, b. Sept. 1, 1894.
639 Guy, b. Jan. 18, 1896.
640 Miles, b. Jan. 5, 1899.
641 Theodore, b. Aug. 9, 1900.

(401)

STEPHEN LONGSTROTH was born Dec. 11, 1870, at Mendon, Utah. Married July 20, 1909, Leva Thomas, daughter of William W. and Annie M. (Barchu) Granger. She was born June 10, 1877, at Marion, Ohio.

(402)

THOMAS MUIR, son of Thomas and Jane Muir, was born April 11, 1872, at Mendon, Utah. Married March 1, ——, Mary Longstroth. She was born Nov. 2, 1872, at Mendon, Utah.

Children: Born at Mendon.
642 Maggie, b. Sept. 2, 1893.
643 Hazel, b. Dec. 26, 1894.
644 Melvin Thomas, b. Aug. 13, 1896.
645 William Gilbert, b. July 19, 1898.
646 Byron L., b. Jan. 24, 1900.
647 Grace, b. Sept. 9, 1903.
648 Armaid Rose, b. March 1, 1906.
649 Stephen L., b. June 7, 1909.

(404)

FREDERICK JAMES MANNING, son of Frederick Charles and Emily (Wilson) Manning, was born ——. Married July 6, 1897, Rosetta Longstroth. She was born Sept. 5, 1876, at Mendon, Utah. Resides at Garland, Utah.

Children: Born at Mendon.
650 Emily, b. April 24, 1899.
651 Alfred, b. Feb. 9, 1902.
652 Blanche, b. Oct. 19, 1904.
653 Hugh, b. Dec. 26, 1906.
654 Louisa, b. Nov. 28, 1908.

(405)

JOHN W. EVANS, son of Hyrum and Ann Evans. Married June 7, 1899, in the Salt Lake Temple, Phoebe Longstroth. She was born Feb. 2, 1879, at Mendon, Utah.
Children: Born in Mendon.
655 Charlotte Ann, b. Jan. 27, 1902.
656 Phoebe, b. July 30, 1903.
657 Alice, b. March 2, 1907.
658 George W., b. May 23, 1909.

(406)

JAMES W. WRIGHT, son of A. R. and Lucy (Warhop) Wright, married June 13, 1907, Sarah Longstroth. She was born Feb. 18, 1892, at Mendon, Utah.
Children:
659 Lucy C., b. Dec. 31, 1908.

(407)

WM. GILL LONGSTROTH was born Sept. 17, 1883, at Mendon, Utah. Married June 12, 1907, in the Logan Temple, Clara May, daughter of Jacob and Susan (Hancock) Sorenson. She was born March 22, 1886, at Mendon, Utah.
Children: Born at Mendon.
660 Phillis, b. June 29, 1908.

(408)

ALFRED THEODORE A. PETERBORG, son of Emil and Eriche (Lundgren) Peterborg. Married Nov. 11, 1908, Allie Longstroth. She was born Dec. 21, 1885, at Mendon, Utah.
Children:
661 Theodore Lynn, b. Sept. 29, 1909, at Idaho.

(409)

ALMA LONGSTROTH, born June 7, 1888, at Mendon, Utah. Married Oct. 11, 1910, Ivy Coburn, daughter of John P. and Anabell Leathan Coburn.

(417)

SPENCER BAKER SHUMWAY was born Aug. 12, 1878, at Richmond, Utah. Residing with his parents until they located at Mesa, Ariz. He married Annie Laura Willis. She was born April 3, 1889. He is a contractor and builder, and manufacturer of cement blocks at Holbrook, Ariz. Residence, Holbrook.
Children:
662 Alvord Le Roy, b. Jan. 24, 1909, d. March 9, 1909.

(419)

JAMES THOMAS ARROWSMITH was born Dec. 23, 1881, at Mesa, Maricopa, Ariz., where he married April 14, 1904, Henrietta, daughter of Spencer D. and Elizabeth (Baker) Shumway. She was born Nov. 30, 1882, at Johnson, Kane County, Utah. He died Aug. 2, 1908, at Mesa, Ariz.
Children:
663 James Lee, b. April 4, 1905, at Mesa, Ariz.

(420)

FREDERICK SINGLETON MADDOX, son of Benjamin Franklin and Perennial Catherine (Clark) Maddox, was born Sept. 10, 1875, in Early County, Georgia. Removed with his parents to Utah and resided for a time at Ogden, Utah. In the latter part of 1904 he removed to Mesa, Ariz., where he soon after married Sarah Elizabeth, daughter of Spencer D. and Elizabeth (Baker) Shumway. She was born Feb. 10, 1885, at Linden, Apache County, Ariz.
Children:
664 Ruth Elizabeth, b. April 4, 1906, at Mesa, Ariz.
665 Viola C., b. Nov. 7, 1908, at Mesa, Ariz.

Note—Benjamin Franklin Maddox was born Aug. 8, 1817, at Limestone County, Ala. Died Aug. 4, 1901.

Perennial Catherine Clark was born Jan. 8, 1852, in Dooley County, Georgia.

JOHN W. WINTLE 427 DAISY L. (STONE) WINTLE 427

(427)

JOHN WESLEY WINTLE, son of Joseph Barney and Mary Marinda (Wilson) Wintle, was born May 20, 1870, at Wilson, Weber County, Utah. He married Aug. 5, 1908, in the Latter Day Saints Temple, at Salt Lake City, Utah, Daisy Louella, daughter of Merlin J. and Maria (Baker) Stone. She was born Dec. 9, 1878, at Ogden, Utah.

Mr. Wintle was a graduate of the Weber Stake Academy at Ogden, and also attended the University of Utah at Salt Lake City. He was a missionary to Germany in 1898 and after his return, taught in the public schools of Weber County two years. He then accepted a position with the Ogden City School Board, with whom he has served as teacher and principal during the last ten years. He holds a teacher's life certificate for Utah and is now (1910) principal of one of the public schools of Ogden.

Mrs. Wintle, when a little over four years old, went with her parents to Beaver Canyon, Idaho, where she received her elementary school training, returning to Ogden in 1890, she continued her course of studies, graduating from the Ogden High School in 1896, and before she was eighteen years of age, had accepted a position as teacher in the Ogden public schools, teaching in the various grades from 1896 to 1910.

In 1903 she and her brother, Merlin, visited the St. Louis Exposition during the summer and also Chicago, returning in time to commence her school in September.

Mr. and Mrs. Wintle now reside in their new home at 878 Twenty-fourth Street, Ogden.

BERTHA MARIA STONE 428

(428)

BERTHA MARIA STONE, daughter of Merlin J. and Maria (Baker) Stone, was born Aug. 15, 1882, at Ogden, Utah. She was educated in the public schools of Ogden, Utah, and was graduated with honors from the Ogden High School in 1900. She was elected class poet by her class, and wrote and delivered the class poem, entitled "The Naughty-naughts."

Following her graduation, she was teacher in the public schools of Ogden, where she was recognized as a young woman of marked ability. During this time she completed a correspondence course in journalism and in 1906 became a member of the editorial staff of the Ogden Standard, serving as telegraph and social editor. Many special articles were also written by her for this paper. In the fall of 1909, Miss Stone accepted a position as teacher in the public schools of Imperial County, California, securing a California life certificate, after passing rigid examinations. She also attended the State Normal School at San Diego.

She is now, 1911, teaching in the city of Imperial, California, with splendid success, and incidentally, is establishing herself as a writer of no mean ability.

THE NAUGHTY NAUGHTS.

Old time is gliding, swiftly speeding by,
   Our happy school life now is truly o'er,
And tears will come when'er our thoughts revert
   To times that have been, but will be no more.

When Latin, German, History, filled the hours
   With toil delectable, though oft severe,
And Mathematics through our brains did drive
   Those mists that even English failed to clear.

Yet come with me and wander back again,
   To that eventful night we've ne'er forgot,
When we were blushing Eighth Grade graduates,
   Upon the brink of graver High School thought.

Oh, what a brilliant future we beheld!
   And how we cherished airy phantoms, dreams!
Our High School life was bright as when the sun
   Doth dissipate the clouds with ardent beams.

We did not think, alas, that all those tasks,
   Those heavy burdens, sighs, and briny tears
Alone would bear us to more lofty heights,
   When we had labored zealously for years.

With swelling hearts we joined the Freshman class,
   And pleasantly the fleeting year was spent—
For though we had so much to overcome,
   Our self-importance conquering power lent.

What self-conceit betrayed a Freshman lad!
   What dignity assumed a Freshman lass!
We almost thought we were the school ourselves—
   That vain delusion haunts each Freshman class.

How can we tell what we so calmly bore
   All through that first and trying High School year!
How those, in wisdom more advanced than we,
   So empty made our tow'ring pride appear.

As time went on and we in wisdom grew,
   Most points of knowledge we discerned with ease,
And could distingish, if we tried real hard,
   A chemical explosion from a sneeze.

But why rehearse the story, long and sad,
   Of blasted hope and other things like that,
'Twere better far, if but my muse permit,
   To tell you who we are, and where we're at.

In number now we boast but twenty-four,
   From ninety-five diminished—what a shrink!
Yet, after what we've been through, 'tis surprise
   To find we are so many, don't you think?

Full many a maid with soft and languid eyes,
   The weak, susceptible young man beguiled,
Full many a marriage made us wonder why
   The Fates had never thus upon us smiled.

And some have wandered far to distant lands,
   With high and noble purposes in view,
To win new converts to their chosen creed—
   While others brisker business life pursue.

But we have struggled on these four years past—
   We see before us now a future bright,
For sure we are a most illustrious class
   Whose fame ascends to many a lofty height.

When peering through the perspective glass of time,
   Across the undulating plain of life,
We see familiar forms of days gone by,
   Reminding us of High School's pleasant strife.

How many of our classmates dear we see
   In busy eddies of professional whirl—
A great physician who, for sweet love's sake,
   Dispatches joyfully the other girl.

A learned minister with visage mild
   Who always gives his blessing for a fee—
The minstrel also of our brilliant class,
   Who leads the choir by popular decree.

A promising young lawyer, grave and wise,
   Whose many clients come from far and wide—
The realistic artist, world renowned,
   Whose comic etchings latent genius hide.

Before us lies a smiling future life,
   Attained by earnest toil and honest work—
Our later lives will surely all reveal
   That we've a duty never tried to shirk.

For even though we've often wearily
   So longed to turn aside from tasks begun,
What strength sublime filled our triumphant souls,
   When we were told our duties were well done.

Now we must leave these pleasant scenes so dear,
   To meet the storms of life, as well as peace;
But through it all we'll surely ne'er forget
   Our motto, "Mens aequa in ardius."

Though we may roam to distant sunny climes,
   We'll yet remember our old High School hall,
Where we were taught so many precious truths,
   Which through our future life we'll oft recall.

'Tis sad to think that we must from thee part—
   But yet we hope our future lives will tell
That we have learned the lessons thou hast taught,
   So Alma Mater, fare thee well, farewell.

                              —BERTHA M. STONE.

EFFIE MAUDE STONE 429

(429)

EFFIE MAUDE STONE, daughter of Merlin J. and Maria (Baker) Stone, was born May 24, 1887, at Beaver Canyon, Idaho. In November, 1890, she moved with her parents to Ogden, Utah, where she has since lived. She received her education in the public schools of Ogden, being graduated in June, 1906, from the Ogden High School. Besides completing with credit the classical course, she mastered the course in stenography, and upon her graduation accepted a responsible position as stenographer and typist.

Miss Stone is now (1911) a valued member of the office of the Pioneer Fruit Company, Sacramento, California, her excellent work in the Ogden office securing for her this enviable position.

MERLIN J. STONE, JR. 430

(430)

MERLIN JONES STONE, JR., son of Merlin J. and Maria (Baker) Stone, was born May 2, 1891, at Ogden, Utah, where he also attended school until he was graduated from the Ogden High School, in June, 1909. He made a splendid record and was chosen by his class to deliver the class oration at the commencement exercises.

In the fall of 1909 he entered as a freshman in the school of mines at the University of Utah. He spent the summer of 1910 in Goldfield, Nevada, where he entered the employ of the Goldfield Consolidated Company, his practical work there providing an invaluable asset for further work in his chosen course. He is now (1911) a sophomore at the University of Utah.

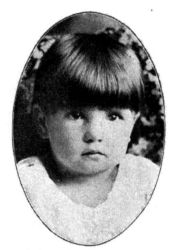

MABEL ELIZABETH STONE 431

(431)

MABEL ELIZABETH STONE, daughter of Merlin J. and Maria (Baker) Stone, and twin sister to her only brother, Merlin J., Jr., was born May 2, 1891, at Ogden, Utah, and died there April 7, 1899.

Mabel Elizabeth was a very ambitious child, very attentive to her studies during the two years of her attendance at school, and her rapid progress seemed to predict a bright future for her, but she was stricken with a severe illness, which baffled the skill of the best physicians, and she passed away.

Little Mabel has gone. Her bright hazel eyes sparkle no more,
Save in rivalry with the stars that are glittering o'er,
In the dome of the mansion that was not made with hands,
Eternal in the heavens. With the angelic bands,
The mission of her lovely soul will mature more sweet,
Than could rugged earth surrender to her tireless feet.

Our sweet little Mabel has left us; our joy and pride;
Called away! She was "Wanted on the other side."
Eight years was the meausre of her life. All is o'er now;
Death has set its icy seal upon her heated brow.
After the unspoken sorrow of anguish. pain and gloom,
She was laid away in the restful shadows of the tomb.

M. J. S.

(522)

WILLIAM S. HASTINGS was born July 20, 1858, at Leydon. Mass. Married March 16, 1880, M. Genevra Miner; she was born Sept. 19, 1861, at Leydon, Mass. About 1904 they removed from Northfield, Mass., to Haines City, Florida, where they now reside.
Children:
666 Leon Severence, b. July 3, 1882, at Brattleboro, Vt., d. July 11, 1901.
667 Geo. Earl, b. July 4, 1884, at Guilford, Vt., m. Gertrude M. Sargent. X
668 Mabel E., b. July 2, 1886, at Guilford, Vt.
669 Raymond M., b. Oct. 9, 1888, at Guilford, Vt.
670 Lillian M., b. Sept. 26, 1890, at Northfield, Mass.
671 Robert F., b. Jan. 11, 1893, at Northfield, Mass.
672 Kenneth W., b. Dec. 3, 1894, at Northfield, Mass.
673 William W., b. Jan. 3, 1897, at Northfield, Mass.
674 Floyd L., b. Nov. 15, 1898, at Norhtfield, Mass
675 Harold H., b. Dec. 4, 1900, at Northfield, Mass
676 Mattie Leona, b. March 29, 1903, at Northfield, Mass.

(534)

JOHN MERITT, married Jan. 1884, Mary Elizabeth, daughter of James and Elizabeth (Shepardson) Lambert. She was born Jan. 11, 1861, at Lyons, Wills Co., Iowa
Children:
677 Grace.

(598)

ROBERT HARVEY, son of Robert B. and Emma (Foerhand) Harvey, was born Nov. 8, 1884, at Mountain View, Uinta County, Wyo., at which place he married Nov. 27, 1907, Ida May, daughter of Thomas Irven and Ida (Bird) Johnson; she was born April 29, 1889, at Dry Fork, Uinta County, Utah.
Children:
678 Robert W., b. Aug. 25, 1908, at Mountain View, Wyo.
679 Harold Leslie, b. Nov. 8, 1909, at Robertson, Wyo.

(599)

GEORGE GRAHAM, son of Bishop James and Jane (Laird) Graham, was born Nov. 21, 1884, at Airdrie, Scotland. Married Jan. 20, 1909, at Robertson, Wyo., Orel Marion, daughter of Thomas Irven and Ida (Bird) Johnson. She was born May 17, 1891, at Dry Fork, Uintah County, Utah.
Children:
680 Ida May, b. Nov. 24, 1909, at Cumberland, Uintah, County, Wyo.

(667)

GEORGE EARL HASTINGS was born July 4, 1884, at Guilford, Vt. Married Jan. 4, 1905, Gertrude May Sargent.
Children:
621 Leon Vern, b. Aug. 19, 1907, at Bartow, Florida.

PART THREE

COLLATERAL BRANCHES

THE HILL FAMILY.

ALEXANDER HILL was a British sailor, tall and slender, very erect, and one of the most nimble and athletic of men. His graphic descriptions of his travels and experiences, which he was constantly relating, would thrill and fill one with wonderment.

Mr. Hill and his wife, whose maiden name was Elizabeth Curry, and their children, viz., Daniel, Agnes, John, Alexander, Mary, Archibald and Elizabeth, came to America about 1819 and established their home in Canada. Their former home was Johnson, not many miles from Glasgow, Scotland. The whole of this family left Ontario, Can., in 1841 or 1842 for the United States, locating first at Nauvoo, Ill., and thence to Utah from 1847 to 1851, where they helped to colonize the new country.

THE LEAVITT FAMILY.

Mr. Leavitt of Hatfield, Quebec, Lower Canada, probably died there before 1837, as this year his wife, together with a number or their children and grand-children joined the Latter Day Saint Church, having been converted by Elder Hazen Eldrigde.

On July 7, 1837, Mrs. Leavitt, who was then 76 years old, and a number of her children and grand-children, consisting of about 35 persons, left their native land to join the Mormon colonies. They traveled through the state of New York and Vermont and two of the families stopped that winter in Ohio. The others went further west, Nathaniel to Michigan and the others to Twelve-Mlie Grove, Ill., at which place Mrs. Leavitt died in 1839. The two families, who, during the winter of 1837-38 had stopped in Ohio, came to Twelve-Mile Grove, the following summer, where they purchased farms, intending to remain there until they learned where the church had settled.

Children:
2 Jeremiah, m. Sarah Studevant.
3 Wiear, m. Abigail Cole.
4 Nathaniel, m. Deborah Dillou.
5 John, m. Lucy Lane.

(2)

JEREMIAH LEAVITT born probably at Hatley, Lower Canada; married Sarah Studevant. He left Canada with the Leavitt colony in 1837 to join the Mormons, locating first in Illinois, and later his children came to Utah. They had eight children, among whom were the following: He died about 1847, with cholera, leaving his family on the prairie, wending their waay westward.

Children.
6 Jeremiah, b. Feb. 10, 1822, in Lower Canada, m. Eliza Harover.
7 Dudley, of St. George, Utah, b. 1829, Lower Canada. Residence, Littlefield, Mohava County, Arizona.
8 Lemuel S., of Santa Clara, Washington County, Utah.
9 Thomas Rowell, b. June 30, 1834, at Compton, Lower Canada.
10 John, of Garland, Utah.

WIEAR LEAVITT was born probably at Hatley, Lower Canada, emigrated with the Leavitt colony, in 1837, to the United States, and Located at Twelve-Mile Grove, Ill., about 40 miles south of Chicago, where he died in 1839. He married first in Canada, Abigail Cole; and second her sister, Phoebe Cole, who came with him to Illinois, and later, together with her children and Mr. Simon Baker's family, to Utah, in 1847.

Children:
11 Jeremiah, d. about 1839 at Twelve-Mile Grove, Ill.
12 Charlotte, b. Dec. 5, 1818, at 'Lower Canada, m. Simon Baker.
13 Louiza, b. at Lower Canada, m. Horton Haaight.
14 George d. at Smithfield, Cache County, Utah.
15 Charles, d. probably at Twelve-Mile Grove, Ill.
Children: Second wife.
16 Emeline, m. Pres. William Smith of Centerville, Utah.

To Whom It May Concern: While the writer has compiled an extensive Leavitt Genealogy, no arrangements have been made to publish it with this volume, but those who may become interested, in this line, may obtain from the writer or his library much more valuable data concerning the Leavitt family.

MERLIN J. STONE,
2869 Grant Ave., Ogden, Utah.

THOMAS ROWELL LEAVITT (See Leavitt Gen.)

THOMAS ROWELL LEAVITT, son of Jeremiah and Sarah (Studevant) Leavitt was born June 30, 1834, at Compton, Quebec, Lower Canada; died May 21, 1891, at Cardston, Canada. He married first, March 1, 1857, Ann Eliza Jenkins of American Fork, Utah. He married second during the winter or early spring of 1861, Antonette Davenport; she died in the fall of 1880. He married third, July, 1883, Harriett Martha Dowdle of College Ward, Cache County, Utah.

Mr. Leavitt was the sixth child of a family of eight, his parents being farmers; his early childhood was on the farm, moving with his parents to the United States when only three years of age, and joined the Mormon colonies in Illinois, and moving with them from place to place westward. His father died in 1847, with cholera, leaving the family with a sick mother on the prairie wending their way westward, sharing the persecutions of "the Saints," many hardships were endured, reducing the family to extreme poverty and depriving the younger members of a scolactic education, but through industry and thrift, the boy won for himself an exceptionaally good education for those days.

Arriving in Utah in the early fiftys they settled in Toole, Utah, where they manged to exist in common with the people of that day. Mr. Leavitt with his young wife moved to Cache Valley in 1857, where he had previously been and erected the first house in Wellsville, but later abandoned this place to take part in the "move south," with the general exodus of the Mormons in the spring of 1858, after which he settled in the Dixie Country on the Santa Clara, the climate not agreeing with his wife, he moved back to Cache Valley, but not until after having filled a one year mission to the Moquish Indians, where he suffered excrutiating pangs of hunger, having to boil, then broil his mocassins for food, after having devoured their only mule.

His many experiences with the Indians proved him to be a man of great courage, showing many evidences of bravery; serving his town as constable for twenty-five years; following the occupation of a farmer, he was able to furnish his numerous family a living and give them a common school education.

On the 21st of March, 1888, he left Cache County, for Alberta, Canada, arriving there the latter part of May, settling on Lee's Creek —now Cardston, and being acquainted with pioneering, he at once commenced building and had the honor of erecting the first house in Cardston. His family were as follows:

His first wife's children, six sons and six daughters; his second wife's children were five sons and four daughters, and the third wife's children were two sons and three daughters, being a total of 13 sons and 13 daughters of whom now (1910) 22 are living.

The country being suited to farming, the spring of 1900 finds all but one of his sons emigrating to the same land and also four of his then five sons-in-law. Twelve sons and six sons-in-law settling in what is now Leavitt, Thomas R. Leavitt having been the pioneer; the town of Leavitt was named in his honor.

His text always yea, a do'er of the law, not merely a hearer. He served as councillor to Cardston's first Bishop until his death; he died as he had lived a true and faithful Latter Day Saint, keeping God's commandments and observing every law as he understood them, leaving a posterity of 300 children, grand-children and great grand-children. To know him was to love him; he died without leaving a known enemy, being sick but a very short time he passed away with la grippe.

THE MOWRY FAMILY.

ALBERT W. MOWRY, Sr., son of Waterman and Sarah (Young) Mowry was born Dec. 31, 1821, at Winfield, Herkermer County, New York. He married Martha E. —— and about 1858-9 removed to Brookfield, N. Y., and engaged in the mercantile business. He also owned a small farm at Brookfield.

He died June 1, 1884, at Brookfield. His wife was administratrix of his estate. She sold the mercantile business and in 1885 was living on their farm at Brookfield.

Children: Born at Winfield.

ALBERT W. MOWRY, JR., was born Aug. 5, 1846, at Winfield. N. Y.; married about 1872, Miss Gertie Greene, of Wets Winfield. He died Feb. 11, 1887, at Utica, N. Y., and was buried at Brookfield.

Mr. Mowry, when a small boy, removed with his parents to Brookfield, N. Y. He received a business education at Eastman's Business University, at Poughkeepsie, and upon leaving that institution commenced busness in the store of his father, where he developed a good reputation, as a business man, and a first rate salesman and bookkeeper.

Mr. and Mrs. Mowry, about the last of December, 1886, removed to Utica, N. Y., and just become comfortably established in their new home when death released him from the troubles and perplexities of life. He left a wife and mother to mourn his death.

MARTHA JANE MOWRY, daughter of Albert W., Sr. and Martha E. Mowry was born Dec. 11, 1850, at Winfield, N. Y. She married Oct. 4, 1869, Joseph W. C. Burdick, and died Jan. 13, 1872, at Milwaukee, Wis.

She was buried at Brookfield, N. Y.; having been brought to her old home a corpse just eight weeks from the time they removed to Wisconsin, where they were intending to engage in business.

THE RICHARDS FAMILY.

The name Richards is of French origin and was no doubt transplanted on British soil, from Normandy, France, in the year 1066, when the Duke of Normandy or William the Conqueror invaded Britian and established himself upon the throne of England.

The name has become anglicized by the addition of a letter "s." There are French speaking villages in Continental Europe, where the most of the population is made up of families called Richard, Dubois and Racine.

(1)

John Richards was born about 1750, in Scotland, where he married A Miss Wilson, whose brother, Wilson, a writer, solicitor or barrister, as the word writer implies, was a reputable and wealthy attorney in Glascow, where he founded the Glascow Infirmary, by endowing it with £5,000 stirling, as evidence by his portrait in life size, which hangs in the reception hall of that institution.

There was issus born of this marriage, seven sons and one daughter. Six of the sons went to the West Indies, where we understand they amassed great fortunes; the sister, Mary Richards, lived in Glascow, and died in the Infirmary, which her uncle had so liberally endowed.

JOHN RICHARDS, eldest son of above, was born at or near Glascow, Scotland, about 1775, and near the beginning of the nineteenth Century, he came to Quebec, Canada, presumably as an artillery man, in the British army. Later he was appointed Commander General of the Royal artillery at Quebec.

About 1804, he married Maria Angeline Kennedy, a French lady; of this union there was born, two sons, John and Thomas, who were born while their father was yet in command at Quebec, the former in 1805, and the latter in about three years later. While the boys were still small, their father was released from his Military service, at Quebec, to return to his home at or near Glascow. The two boys were brought up and received very good educations, considering the times in which they lived.

The General and his wife separated and he married second, a Miss Hamilton, of the town of Hamilton, in the suburban district of Glascow. Miss Hamilton was of the ancient family, bearing that name, and claimed the distinction of being one of the nobility of Scotland.

The two boys lived with their father and step-mother, at Hamilton. Mrs. Hamilton Richards had born to her of this marriage, a number of children, one daughter of whom married a Mr. Bar, and has two sons, now in easy circumstances, living near the West End Park, of Glascow. Another daughter, Mary, married Thomas Lindsay; they had a large family; Mr. Lindsay died about 1907, at Motherwell. Mrs. Lindsay, together with most of her family, lives in the little town of Motherwell, not many miles from Glascow. She is a good and comely woman, resembling somewhat, her half-brother, John.

General John Richards and his son, Thomas, both died at Hamilton, and presumably were buried there, though we have failed to locate their tombs.

JOHN RICHARDS, son of Gen. John Richards, was born May 16, 1805, at Quebec, Canada, and while quite young went with his father to Scotland, residing for some time with his father and stepmother, at Hamilton, near Glascow. When fifteen years of age, he returned to Quebec, Canada. Here he grew to manhood, and being of a studious nature, learned to speak French, and took great pride in becoming a grammarian and mastering the English language.

About 1830, at Quebec, Canada, he married Agnes, daughter of Alexander and Elizabeth (Curry) Hill; she was born June 6, 1808, at Johnson, 25 miles from Glascow, Scotland. They were reputed to be the most handsome couple from far and near in the neighborhood where they lived.

John Richards' weight was 160 to 170 pounds, complexion dark, was endowed with an iron constitution and was remarkably athletic. He partook more of the nature of his French mother; his temperament varying at times; frequently communicative; continually talking of his relatives and friends and relating his experiences; was an inveterate reader, knew as it were "King James" translation of the bible from start to finish. He was qiute conversant with the poets, Burns and Scott, judging from his frequent quotation from them.

At other times he was extremely reticent, whole days passing without his speaking a word, except in case of necessity, and exhibiting a marked degree of patience. He was extremely honest in his business transactions in life; the law of prescription or statute of limitations had no place in his code of ethics; he paid his debts regardless of sacrifice, as soon as he could, no matter if seven or seven and twenty years time might have intervened, and took great pleasure in settling his obligations.

Agnes Hill Richards was proportionate in build, weighed 140 pounds, complexion blond, was more uniform in temperament, and had a very forcible manner of speech; her character was just as sterling as that of her husband, and her honesty of purpose was never qestioned, and she like her husband was always ready to help the needy and succor the distressed.

Their first child, Elizabeth, at three years of age had been taught to speak English and French and her dancing was fine for that age; a kettle of maple syrup had been placed on a log fire, for the purpose of making sugar; the log burned through, the kettle fell and the three year old child who was playing on the hearth received the boiling contents and died almost immediately.

About 1833 the family moved to Ontario, Upper Canada, where the family had the misfortune to have their home destroyed by fire.

About 1840, an Elder of the Latter Day Saint Church, a Mr. Samuel Lake, who was a ready speaker and an excellent scriptorian, came to this place and was soon successful in converting all of the Richards and Hill families to that faith, with the exception of John Richards, who took more time to consider the doctrine, but later when he did embrace the Gospel, he would have permitted the last drop of his heart blood to leak out in sacrifice, rather than renounce the faith he had espoused.

In 1841 or 1842, the Richards family, together with the Hill families migrated to the United States and settled at Nauvoo, Ill., here they suffered the persecutions in common with the rest of the Mormons.

One instance worthy of note may be mentioned: John Richards, Daniel, John, Archibald, and perhaps Alexander Hill, a Baptist Minister and two others were harvesting wheat near Nauvoo, when, during the day, some 40 ruffians, dressed in disguise, in women's apparel, passed by in the woods near where they were working; remarks were made as to why so many women should be passing by in that section of the country, when John Richards said: "It is a Mob; they are men; I can hear the clinking of their big boots." This proved to be correct, for in less than an hour the same "Mobocrats" came back, in men's clothing, disarmed the eight harvesters, broke their fire arms to pieces, and cutting a number of hickory withes, three of four feet in lenkth and nearly an inch in diameter, compelled the laborers, at the point of the bayonet, to lay bare to the waist, and then proceeded to flog them; they stood their victims in a dyke, some three feet deep, with their stomachs lying across the bank, there to receive twenty strokes of the hickory cudgel across and upon their nude backs, with a fresh man from their number to weild the cudgel for each victim.

Mr. Richards after having taken his medicine patiently, returned a complacent smile of thanks, which was construed as a derisive smile, and came near subjecting him to another round of torture, but on the suggestion of one of their number, that he had received enough he was permitted to go.

When it came the Baptist's turn, he entered a plea that he was not a Mormon, and should not be whipped; he was informed, that like poor dog tray, he was found in bad company, and must take his medicine.

John Richards established himself a home in the city of Nauvoo, and was on the way to prosperity, when soon after the death of the prophet, Joseph Smith when so many of the leaders of the Church were compelled to leave Naauvoo, he haveing good teams, was called to assist them in moving. Accordingly he went, leaving his family at Nauvoo, he took his teams and with a load of Brigham Young's goods and in company with Brigham Young, Dr. Willard Richards and others wended their way westward into the wilderness.

He returned to Nauvoo, and in the summer of 1846, he and his family were driven from Nauvoo, and compelled to cross the Mississippi river near Montrose, Lee County, Iowa, on July 27th., and three or four days later were compelled to move up the river, on account of the hostility of the mob. From there they removed to Honey Creek, Iowa, and there remained until the spring of 1851, when the family began their journey for the Great Salt Lake, with Luman Shurtliff as captain of the ten, experiencing the usual hardships common with the emigrants of that time, they arrived at Salt Lake City the latter part of September, or early in October, 1851, and settled on Mill Creek, a few miles south of Salt Lake City.

In 1857, on the approach of Johnston's army, their son, John, enlisted with the "Mormon" army and spent part of that year in Echo Canyon, and the family removed to Santaquin, Utah, returning to Mill Creek the following year of 1858, and their sons, John Joseph and Hyrum went to Mendon, Cache Valley, to locate farms, and on Christmas day, 1859, the rest of the family arrived at Mendon and another home was established.

Mr. Richards died Nov. 15, 1884, at Mendon, Cache County, Utah.

Mrs. Richards died March 30, 1886, at Mendon, Cache County, Utah.

Children:

Elizabeth, b. about 1831, d. aged 3 years.
Thomas, died at birth.
Elizabeth, b. July 22, 1835, at Ontario, Canada, m. Manning Rowe.
Mary, b. May 15, 1837, at Ontario, Canada, m. James P. Terry.
John, b. June 2, 1839, at Ontario, Canada, d. s.
Joseph, b. Dec. 5, 1841, at Ontario, Canada, m. Mary Willie.
Agnes, b. Nov. 1, 1843, at Nauvoo, Ill, m. Geo. W. Baker. (123)
Rachel, b. July 27, 1846, near Montrose, Iowa, m. Jarvis Baker. (119)
Hyrum Thomas, b. March 22, 1849, Honey Creek, Iowa, m. Agnes Muir Findley.
Alex. Willard Hill, b. Oct. 10, 1851, Mill Creek, Salt Lake County, m. Sena Sorenson.
Daniel Brigham, b. Nov. 14, 1853, Mill Creek, m. Marie Sorenson.

SHEPARDSON LINEAGE.

(1)

JOHN SHEPARDSON, born 1718, died 1798, at Brattlebrough, Vermont.
Children:
3 Zephana, b. May 6, 1733.

(2)

DANIEL SHEPARDSON, brother of John (1) was born 1728, married Mary ——. She was born about 1730.
Children:
4 Noah.

(3)

ZEPHANA SHEPARDSON born May 6, 1733, and married Ruth, daughter of Samuel and Mary Hills. She died in Ellisburg, N. Y., 1884, aged 94 years, 10 months.
Children: Born in Attleborough, Mass.
5 Zephana, b. March 21, 1755, m. Rachel ——. X.
6 William, b. July 25, 1756, m. Grace ——. X.
7 Ruth, b. Sept. 16, 1758.
8 Joseph, b. Oct. 27, 1760, m. Zurvier Packer. X.
9 Jared, b. July 8, 1762, d. unm., aged 48.

(5)

ZEPHANA SHEPHARDSON, born March 21, 1755, at Attleborough, Mass., married Rachel ——, who was born 1755, and died Sept. 28, 1787. He married second, Letice ——. They had 16 children, among whom were the following:
Children:
10 Sallay, m. —— Barney, d. about 1883, aged 94 years 10 months.
11 Zephana.
12 James.
13 Clark, d. 1886, in Milwaukee, aged 81 years.

(6)

WILLIAM SHEPARDSON born July 25, 1756, married Grace ——.
Children:
14 Thaddeus, died of consumption.
15 Cynthis, died of consumption.
16 Hart, died of consumption.
17 Polly, died of consumption.

(8)

JOSEPH SHEPARDSON was born Oct. 27, 1760, at Attleborough, Mass. He married in Guilford, Vt., Oct. 25, 1787, Zurvier

Packer (see Packer lineage). She died Oct. 7, 1806, at Leydon, Mass., aged 38 years. He died Nov. 2, 1821, at Colerain, Mass.
Children:
18 Jared, b. May 9, 1788, at Guilford, Vt., m. Aug. 2, 1812, at Zanesville, Ohio, Matilda Denison. He died Oct. 11, 1825, at Monroe, Ohio. They had six children.
19 Rebecca, b. May 3, 1790, m. April 27, 1809, Calvin Weld, res. Coventry, N. Y.
20 Zurvier, b. March 9, 1792, m. April 5, 1810, at Leydon, Mass., Benj. S. Grimell, 10 children, res. Harpersville, Ohio.
21 Joseph, b. Feb. 22, 1794, Leydon, Mass., d. 1841, Dresdon, O.,
22 Lucinda, b. Dec. 12, 1795, m. Feb. 9, 1818, Ezra Babcock, 3 children She died aged 88 years
23 William Henry, b. April 17, 1797, m. Mary Baker (46).
24 James Packer, b. May 7, 1799, m. and died Oct. 24, 1834, at Sandusky, Ohio.
25 Horatio Jefferson, b. Dec. 28, 1800, m. Feb. 28, 1827, at Colerain, Mass., Mary S. Brown. He died Nov. 15, 1886, at Greenfield, Mass. Five children.
26 Salome, b. Aug. 25, 1803, m. Dec. 16, 1822, at Colerain, Mass., Walter Bell. Six children.

For other Shepardson descendants, see Baker Gen. Part No.2.

SHERMAN LINEAGE.

1 HENRY SHERMAN, born in England; died there.
 Children:
2. Henry Sherman, born in England, lived in Dedham, where he probably died.
 Children.
3 Samuel, born in Dedham, England.
 Children:
4 Philip Sherman, born Feb. 5, 1610, Dedham, Eng.
5 Capt. John Sherman, born Feb., 1613, Dedham, Eng.

(4)

PHILIP SHERMAN was born Feb. 5, 1610, at Dedham, England, and died 1687, at Portsmouth, R. I. He married Sarah, daughter of Mr. and Mrs. Margaret Odding.

In 1633 he came to Massachusetts and soon settleed in Roxbury. Made Freeman, May 14, 1634. On November 20th, 1637, he and others were warned to deliver up all guns, pistols, swords, powder, shot, etc., because the "opinions of Mr. Wheelwright and Mrs. Hutchinson have seduced into dangerous errors many of the people here in New England."

March 7, 1638, he and eighteen others signed the following compact:

"We, whose names are underwritten, do here solemnly in the presence of Jehovah incorporate ourselves into a body Politic and as he shall help will submit our persons lives and estate unto our Lord, Jesus Christ, the King of Kings, and the Lord of Lords, and to all the perfect and most absolute laws of his given us in His holy word of truth, to be guided and judged thereby."

March 12, 1638, he and others having to depart from Massachusetts, summons was ordered to go out for them to appear, if they be not gone before, at the next Court, to answer such things as shall be objected.

May 13, 1638, he was present at a general meeting held at portsmouth upon public notice.

1639, Secretary.

1640, he and four others were chosen to lay out land.

1641, March 16, Freeman.

1648 to 1651, General Recorder.

1655, Freeman.

1655 to 1657, Deputy.

April 4, 1676, it was "voted that in these troublesome times and straights in this colony, this assembly desiring to have the advice and concurrence of the most judicious inhabitants, if it may be had for the good of the whole, do desire at their next sitting the company and council of sixteen persons." Among them was Philip Sherman.

Will made July 30, 1681, proved March 23, 1687, Executor, son Samuel, to wife Sarah, use of fire room in west end of dwelling house, a bed and maintenance by son, Samuel, in raiment and necessaries, and to her ten good ewe sheep, kept by executor. To eldest son, Eber, 10 acres in Portsmouth, and what he has had and my horse flesh in Nargansett, except one mare, the second best, which I give to Thomas and Peleg Mumford, my grandchildren. To son, Peleg, five ewe sheep. To son, Edmund, a greater share of meadow and a sixth share of up-land in Ponegansett, in Dartmouth, and also a whole purchase right is Westerly. To son, Samson, at death of wife, the west half of farm I dwell on. To son, Samuel, the rest of farm and my now dwelling house and other buildings and to have two parts of the grass and hay during life with wife, and all meat, cattle, horse kind, sheep and swine, except two and a fattening cow, and all movable goods, except two great chests with lock and key each, which are for wife, Sarah. To son, Samson, a white faced mare with her foal, and those four Indians which we jointly bought. To son, Samsom, and Samuel, my draft horses and two draft steers equally. To son, John, my bay mare and her foal. To son, Benjamin, all the remaining part of my land at Briggs Swamp, where said Benjamin's house now stands, about 20 acres. To daughter, Sarah, 10 ewe sheep. To daughter, Hannah, £5 for hereslf and children, and 5 ewe sheep. To daughter, Phillip, 10 ewe sheep. To son, Edmund, is given Benjamin Chase's son till of age, and he is to be kept in food and clothes till then.

Children:

6 Eber, b. 1634, d. 1706, m. Mary, lived in Kingston, R. I.
7. Sarah, b. 1636, m. Thos. Mumford, d. 1692.
8 Peleg, b. 1638, d. 1719, m. Elizabeth Lawton.
9 Mary, b. 1639, d. y.
10 Edmnd, b. 1641, d. 1719, m. Dorcas ———.
11 Samson, b. 1642, d. June 27, 1718, m. March 4, 1675, Isabel Tripp, b. 1651, d. 1716.
12 William, b. 1643, d. y.
13 John, b. 1644, d. April 16, 1734, m. Sarah Spooner, b. Oct. 5, 1653, d. 1720.
14 Mary, b. 1645, m. Samuel Wilbur, b. 1663, d. 1696.
15 Hannah, b. 1647, m. Wm. Chase, d. 1737.
16 Samuel, b. 1648, d. Oct. 9, 1717, m. Feb. 23, 1681, Martha Tripp, b. 1658, d. 1717.
17 Benjamin, b. 1650, d. Sept. 24, 1719, m. Hannah Mowry, b. Sept. 28, 1656, d. 1718.
18 Phillip, b. Oct. 1, 1652, m. Benjamin Chase, son of Wm. and May Chase, b. 1639, d. 1731.

(5)

CAPT. JOHN SHERMAN was born 1613, in Dedham, England. Came to America, 1634, died Jan. 25, 1691.
Children:
19 Joseph.
19½ Samuel.   —(6).

EBER SHERMAN was born about 1634 at Roxbury, Mass., and went with his parents in childhood to Portsmouth, R. I. He married Mary —— and settled in Kingston, R. I., where he died, 1706.
Children: Probably born in Kingston.
20 Eber.
21 Samuel.
22 Stephen.
23 Elisha.
24 William.
25 Peleg.
26 Abigail.   (19)

JOSEPH SHERMAN.
Children:
27 Nathaniel, b. Sept. 19, 1696.

(23)

ELISHA SHERMAN, son of Eber, of whom but little is known, married and among his children was:
28 Mary, who married Benjamin Baker (24), see Baker Gen.

(27)

NATHANIEL SHERMAN, born Sept. 19, 1696, at Watertown, Mass., married March 31, 1726, Mary Livermore, who was born Dec., 1702.
Children:
29 Asaph, b. Mar. 6, 1741.

(29)

ASAPH SHERMAN was born March 6, 1741, Watertown, Mass. Married July 14, 1762, Lucy Whitney.
Children:
30 Lucy, b. Oct. 25, 1766, m. Job Straw. They were the grand parents of Ambros Shaw, who came to Utah, 1847.

(19)

HON. SAMUEL SHERMAN, son of Capt. John (5) resided at Woodbury, Conn., and among his children was:
31 Sarah, who died March 30, 1712, aged 58 years. She married Josiah Rossiter. They had 17 children, among whom was Sarah, their eleventh child, born Feb. 21, 1691, and married May 9, 1716, Abraham Pierson, who died May 8, 1852, at Killingworth, Conn.

THE SHUMWAY FAMILY.

CHARLES SHUMWAY was born Aug. 1, 1806, at Oxford, Mass., and died May 21, 1898, at Shumway, Arizona. He married in 1832, Julia Ann Hooker; emigrated to Illinois five or six years later. He joined the Latter Day Saints Church, in 1841, and soon after removed to Nauvoo, Ill. During the five years of his residence there, he filled two missions, one to the Cherokee Nation, and the other to Massachusetts. Part of the time he worked on the Latted Day Saint Temple, at Nauvoo, and served also on the police force there.

On leaving Nauvoo for the west he was captain of fifty, and was the very first person to cross the Mississippii river, during the exodus from Illinois. He buried his wife and one daughter at winter quarters. He traveled with President Young's pioneer company until they arrived in the Salt Lake Valley, July, 1847. He was a pioneer to Sanpete Valley in 1849, built the first sawmill there, and was elected a member of the first Legislative Assembly at Salt Lake City, from San Pete County, in 1851.

He removed to Payson where he built another sawmill and later, in 1854, removed to South Cottonwood, Salt Lake County, thence in 1859 to Cache Valley, locating first in Wellsville, and afterwards removed to Mendon. In 1877 he removed to Johnson, Kane County, Utah, and two or three years later to Taylor, Arizona, where he built his last mill.

His death was the second one recorded of the twenty-eight survivers of the Pioneers of Utah, located during the Jubilee of 1897; of the 28 he was the oldest. He left when he died, two living wives and was the father of 35 children.

THE STAPLES FAMILY.

HENRY STAPLES of Bath, England, married there Ann Taylor; she died at Woster, Wostershire, England. He died about 1817, at Red Morley, England.

Children: Born at Bath, England.
Richard, b. 1796.
James, b. January, 1810.

JAMES STAPLES, son of Henry (1) was born Jan., 1810, at Bath, England; died at Salt Lake City, Utah, during the summer of 1874. He married April 12, 1831, at Cheltenham, Gloustershire, England, Sarah, daughter of Richard and Elizabeth (Fable) Limerick; she was born Aug. 14, 1804, at Cheltenham, a town in Gloustershire, with a market on Thursday. Here is a mineral spring, celebrated for its salubrity; and two miles east of the town is another of the same kind. It is nine miles N. E. of Glouster, and 94 W. by N. of London; she died May 24, 1889, at Elsinore, Utah. Mr. Staples came from England to Utah in 1851 and located at Salt Lake City.

The following members of Mr. Staples' family set sail on the 6th day of February, 1852, from Liverpool, England, for New Orleans, in the ship, Ellen Maria, of 768 tons register burden, as shown by their contract ticket, now in the possession of the writer.

Sarah Staples, age 47; Ann Staples, age 20; Elizabeth Staples, age 14; James Staples, age 12½; Henry Staples, age 9½.

Their son, George, came to America in 1847. Mr. Staples was a mason by trade, and worked for many years as mason foreman for President Brigham Young in Salt Lake City.

Children: Born at Cheltenham, England.
4 Ann, b. April 3, 1832, m. Simon Baker. (See Baker Gen.)
5 George, b. June 8, 1835, m. Laura Rapleye.
6 Elizabeth, b. Jan. 8, 1838, m. Simon Baker.
7 James, b. Feb. 15, 1841, m. Sarah ——.
8 Henry, b. Dec. 11, 1844, m. Mary ——.

STILLMAN LINEAGE.

1 Mr. —— Stillman married —— Noyes, a sister of Prudence Noyes, who married Henry Thorn.
Children:
2 Willet.
3 Noyes, m. Tacy Saunders.
4 Surviah, m. —— Wells.
5 Semantha, m. —— Main.
6 Fannie, m. —— Wilcox.
7 Luanna, m. —— Clark.
8 Welcome.
9 Mathew.
10 Caroline, m. —— Bevin.
11 George, unm.
All died previous to 1883, except the last two who were then living.

(3)

NOYES STILLMAN was born probably in Connecticut. He married Tacy Saunders, daughter of Stephen Saunders, who was a son of Stephen Saunders, of Westerly, R. I. They settled at Unadilla Forks, where they lived until the fall of 1862, when they removed to New Brunswick, N. J., and the following spring he bought a farm and died there, Nov., 1866, of heart disease. After settling up their affairs, Mrs. Stillman went to live with their daughter, Ellen Mallen, near North Clymer, Chautauque County, N. Y., where she died in June, 1876.
Children:
12 Samuel N., b. Aug. 5, 1826.
13 William, b. Feb. 21, 1831. He and family moved to Saginaw, Mich., where he was accidently killed. His widow and children, in 1879, were living with her father, Nathan Biand, at Ilion, N. Y.
14 Ellen, m. Alphonse Mallen, res. North Clymer, N. Y.
15 Willet, m., res. Madison, Wis.

(12)

SAMUEL N. STILLMAN was born Aug. 5, 1826, married and settled at Unadilla Forks, Herkimer County, N. Y., where he resided until the spring of 1862, when he removed to New Brunswick, N. J., and where his wife died April 9, 1889.
Children: Born at Unadilla Forks.
16 Elinor Catherine, b. March 18, 1850, m. W. E. Stevenson. Divorced.
17 Helen Eunice, b. Dec. 29, 1851, m. Sept. 10, 1874, Daniel A. Mount.
18 Otto Oseoli, b. April 12, 1854, m. Nov., 1878, ——.
19 Noyes Granville, b. Nov. 12, 1855, m. January, 1879.

COAT OF ARMS—STONE FAMILY

In the Church of St. Mary de Holm-by-the-Sea, against the East pillar of the nave, a mural monument stands, bearing the effigies of a man and his wife; behind him are seven sons, and behind her six daughters—all kneeling with the Arms of Stone-Argent. These are three cinque-foils sable, a chief azure, impaling-barry of six argent and sable, a band over all azure. The Epitapth, translated from the original Latin, is as follows: "Here, underneath, lyeth Richard Stone and Clemens, his wife, who lyved in wedlock joyfully together 64 years and 3 montas. From them proceeded 7 sons and 6 daughters; and from them and theirs issued 72 children, which the sayde Richard and Clemens, to their great comfort, did behold."

THE STONE FAMILY.

REV. SAMUEL STONE, a non-conformist divine, of Hereford, Herefordshire, Engalnd.
Children: Born probably at Hereford.
2 William.
3 John.

(2)

WILLIAM STONE was born about 1608 at Hereford, England. He was one of the original settlers of Guilford, Conn., in 1639. (See Hist. Guilford.) He married first Hannah ——; second Mrs. Mary Hughes. He died 1683 at Guilford.
Children:
4 William, b. 1642; m. Hannah Wolfe.
5 Hannah, b. 1644; m. John Norton.
6 Benajah, b. 1649; m. Hester Kirby.

(4)

WILLIAM STONE was born 1642 at Guilford, Conn. Died there Sept. 28, 1730. Married first Feb. 20, 1664, Hannah, daughter of Edward Wolfe of Lynn, Mass. She died March 28, 1712. He married second Mary ——. She died July 6, 1732.
Children: Born at Guilford.
7 Samuel, b. March 15, 1675; d. April 8, 1675.
8 William, b. March 22, 1676; m. Sarah Hatch.
9 Hannah, b. July 27, 1678; m. William Leete.
10 Daniel, b. July 27, 1680; d. May 16, 1767; m. Elizabeth Talmage.
11 Elizabeth, Nov. 20, 1682; m. Joseph Bishop.
12 Josiah, b. May 22, 1685; d. Dec. 24, 1753; m. Temperance Osborn.
13 Stephen, b. March 1, 1690; m. Elizabeth Leman.
14 Joshua, b. May 3, 1692; m. Susannah Parmelee.
15 Abigail, b. Dec. 1, 1697; m. Nathaniel Bishop.

(8)

WILLIAM STONE was born at Guilford, Conn., March 22, 1676. Died there Sept. 21, 1753. Married Oct. 28, 1701, Sarah Hatch of Guilford. She was born 1681 and died Nov. 26, 1751.
Children: Born at North Guilford.
16 Ezra, b. June 12, 1703; d. July 18, 1703.
17 Jehiel, b. Nov. 11, 1704.
18 Thankful, b. June 10, 1708; d. y.
19 Thankful, b. June 25, 1710; d. Aug. 13, 1729; m. Daniel Hubbard.
20 Daniel, b| Aug. 29, 1711; d. Dec. 23, 1782; m. Leah Norton.
21 Reliance, b. Sept. 24, 1712; d. April 1, 1757; m. Abraham Bradley.
22 Zerojah, b. July 14, 1715; d. Jan. 8, 1769; m. John Hubbard.
23 Ezra, b. July 14, 1717; d. March 20, 1798; m. Elizabeth Osborn.
24 Beata, b. June 26, 1723; d. July 27, 1727.

(15)

JEHIEL STONE was born Nov. 11, 1704, at North Guilford, Conn. He married first at Guilford, Sarah ——. She died Nov. 8, 1728, at Guilford, aged 20. He married second, June 10, 1730, Ruth, daughter of Daniel and Susanah (Mould) White. She was born Sept. 28, 1703, at Middletown, Conn., and died March 28, 1774, at North Guilford.

Children: Born at North Guilford, Conn.
25 Thomas, b. March 16, 1731; m. Leah Norton.
26 Sarah, b. Sept. 2, 1732; d. at New Durham; m. Nov. 5, 1756, Daniel Norton.
27 Elihu, b. Aug. 16, 1734, at Litchfield, Conn.; married Sept. 2, 1755, Thankful Hotchkiss.
28 Ruth, b. March 23, 1736; d. at E. Haven, Conn.; m. Daniel Clark.
29 Noah, b. June 23, 1738; d. Dec. 18, 1745, at Guilford.
30 William, b. Jan. 23, 1740; d. at Harwinton, Conn.
31 Aaron, b. Oct. 21, 1741; d. Jan. 7, 1824, at North Madison; m. Lois Dudley.
32 Isaac, b. Feb. 25, 1743.
33 John, b. Sept. 2, 1744; d. at Guilford, Feb. 15, 1745.
34 Noah, b. 1746.
35 John, b. 1749; m. Mary Parmlee; moved to Ohio.

(30)

ISAAC STONE was born Feb. 25, 1743, at North Guilford, Conn., and died April 25, 1826, at East Bloomfield, N. Y. Married Nov. 4, 1767, Parthena, daughter of Dea. David and Mary (Talman) Dudley. She was born 1750 and died April 25, 1826, at East Bloomfield, N. Y.

Children: Born at North Madison, Conn.
36 Ruth, b. May 28, 1768; d. March 26, 1851; m. Asaph Woodruff, 1790.
37 David Talman, b. Oct. 9, 1769; m. Sept. 29, 1792, Thankful Smith.
38 Parthena, b. July 19, 1771; m. William Cox.
39 Isaac White, b. May 21, 1773; d. Sept. 25, 1814, at Batavia, N. Y.; married Pattie Priest.
40 Parnal, b. June 25, 1775; d. at Bloomfield; m. James Bradley.
41 Amos Sheldon, b. July 22, 1777.
42 Mary, b. May 15, 1779; d. at Epsom, Vt.; m. —— Tyler.
43 Lois, b. Sept. 25, 1781; m. Fred Penoyer.
44 John Jarvis, b. May 1, 1786; m. July, 1823, Caroline Wall.
45 Sophia, m. James Bradley of Canandagua, N. Y.
46 Zerojah, m. Joel Harte.
47 Sally, m. William Lake of Gorham.

AMOS SHELDON STONE was born July 21, 1877, at North Madison, Conn. Died Nov. 28, 1836, at Stockbridge, Mass. He mar-

ried April 19, 1801, at Canaan, N. Y., Rachel, daughter of Daniel and Keziah (Dean) Pease; she was born there Sept. 9, 1780, and died May
   Children:
17, 1851, at Richmond, Mass.
   48 Isaac Dudley, b. Aug. 17, 1802, at Cazenovia, N. Y.; m. Elizabeth Gray.
   49 Daniel Dean, b. Aug. 26, 1804, at Canaan, N. Y.; m. Celestia Thorp.
   50 Lewis Brumley, b. Sept. 1, 1806, at Canaan, N. Y.; m. Lydia B. Waters.
   51 Keziah, b. March 9, 1810, at Canaan, N. Y.; married Charles Webster.
   52 Phineas Cook, b. Sept. 18, 1812; m. Elizabeth Hoyt Tyler.
   53 Amos Pease, of whom hereafter.
   54 John Beebe, b. July 26, 1817, at West Stockbridge, Mass.; m. Mrs. Place.
   55 Rachel Elizabeth, b. Sept. 13, 1820, at Stockbridge; m. Lambert L. Hitchcock.
   56 George Williams, b. Sept. 12, 1822, at West Stockbridge; m. Lucy Webster.
   57 William Edwards, b. Sept. 11, 1825, at Nausau, N. Y.; married Emma E. Murphy.

(51)

AMOS PEASE STONE was born March 18, 1815, at Canaan, Columbus County, N. Y. Died March 17, 1890, at Ogden, Utah. Married Feb. 1, 1846, at Hamden, Conn., Minerva Leantine, daughter of Merlin and Roxana (Ives) Jones. She was born June 4, 1822, at Wallingford, Conn., and died Aug. 17, 1867, at Ogden, Utah.

Mrs. Stone was a conscientious and pious person from early childhood, and was an adept at poetry and artistic work. At the age of 17 she composed the following lines, and wrote them in an autograph album, which in 1887 was in possession of Harriet Jacobs, of Hamden, Conn.:

> Go little volume like the bee,
>   The fertile fields of mind explore,
> 'Till from each mental shrub and tree,
>   Some grateful sweets to fill thy store.
>
> Go and in friendships hallowed name,
>   Where e'er thy wanderings may be,
> An idea fond from feelings claim,
>   A few brief lines from memory.
>   —MINERVA JONES.
> Hamden, Conn., Feb. 2, 1839.

She became a member of the Baptist Church November, 1842, and resigned from the same February 24, 1844. On March 3, 1844, she joined the Latter Day Saints Church, being the first convert from her father's family.

March 20, 1846, she left her native state to move west with the Mormons, Mr. Stone leaving there on the 22nd, joined his family the same day at Philadelphia, Pa. Resuming their journey on March 27th, they arrived at Nauvoo, Ill., May 11, and on July 5 following they started again for the west and arrived at Council Bluffs, Iowa, July 15, 1846, just as the last company of volunteers were preparing to leave for the Mexican war.

They first located at Kanesville, and the following spring of 1847 they removed to Mosquito Creek, where they built a two-room log house on a small farm and raised buckwheat and corn and made maple sugar.

During the summer of 1846 Mr. Stone returned to Connecticut on a visit, returning in the fall with Mrs. Stone's parents and family.

On October 11, 1848, Mrs. Stone wrote in her journal the following:

"We were counseled to keep a gun in the house constantly, as they feared an attack from the Omahas (Indians) and the next day she wrote: "Brother Lee starts for the valleys; he takes with him my rifle, six-shooter, spyglass and their fixtures."

Mrs. Stone also let Joseph Young take a yoke of black oxen to move with to the valleys and they were returned to her Oct. 19, having traveled within 200 miles of the Great Salt Lake; she states in her journal of that date: "Brother Joseph Young returned my oxen to me, which were very poor in flesh and the wagon an interesting monument of the hardships it has endured in this enterprising cause."

In June, 1850, they left the Missouri River for the valleys of the mountains, their outfit consisting of two wagons, three yoke of oxen and one yoke of cows, Mrs. Stone driving one of the teams most of the way.

Mr. Stone did the general blacksmithing for the company, and having studied the Thomsonian System of medicine, he now had a chance to test his medical skill, as cholera broke out in their company; he treated successfully all cases placed in his charge.

They saw thousands of buffaloes while crossing the plains, and one day the sight of an immense herd of buffalo stampeded their ox teams, which ran at a dangerous speed for a long distance. Mrs. Stone at the time was driving next to the head team.

They arrived at the Platte River on July 4th, where their company of fifty divided into three companies for the purpose of traveling faster. The first and last companies formed into one; Captain York of the first ten and their captain, Captain Charles C. Rich of the fifth ten. Captain Harmon Pierson, Captain Leonard and Captain John Carter were captains of the other three tens.

They arrived at Grand Island, 237 miles on their journey on July 16 and at Sweet Water Sept. 11, Fort Bridger Sept. 22 and at Great Salt Lake City Sept. 30, 1850, and five days later located at Sessions

Settlement (Bountiful), ten miles north of Salt Lake City. In March, 1857, they removed to Ogden, Utah, where they made their permanent home.
Children:
58 Olive Ann, b. April 8, 1847, at Council Bluffs, Iowa; married Joseph Parry.
59 Amos Ives, b. Sept. 1, 1849, at Council Bluffs, Iowa; married Emilar Webb.
60 Minerva Pease, b. Nov. 29, 1851, at Bountiful, Utah; married Ambrose Shaw.
61 Merlin Jones, b. Nov. 26, 1853, at Bountiful, Utah; m. Maria Baker.
62 Cordelia H., b. May 21, 1856, at Bountiful, Utah; d. Feb. 18, 1858, at Ogden.
63 Sylvia, b. July 11, 1859, at Ogden, Utah, Utah; m. Irvin T. Alvord.
64 Friend, b. Jan. 5, 1862, at Ogden; m. Josephine Johnson.
65 Vincy Rice, b. Jan. 16, 1864, at Ogden, Utah; m. James John Barker.

THORN LINEAGE.

1. ISAAC THORN, the earliest of the name that we trace to, was born in England, and came to America about the time of the old French and Indian war. He settled in Rhode Island, where he married —— Crandall. She was a large woman and he was a small man. He was a shoemaker and while at work one night at his trade, he had occasion to go outside the house, and never came back. They made all possible search for him, but no trace could be found. They lived by the seashore, where ships came into the bay or river.

After he had been gone a long time, a rumor came by a vessel from the West Indies, that he was alive, and giving a long and full account of his captivity and sufferings. He was seized at his own door by a gang of Freebooters, gagged and carried on board a ship lying near, and thence taken to one of the West India Islands, where this gang of robbers had a cave, where they secreted their plunder; they had a large amount of money, mostly in Spanish Doubloons and other Spanish coins; he tried to get away, but could not without endangering his life. At last an opportunity presented itself. He got free from the gang, and got to Cuba, when he was suddenly taken sick. Believing that he was poisoned, and could not recover, he made arrangements that in some way this report came to his wife, and he was never heard from afterwards.

Children:
2 Henry, b. 1759, in Rhode Island.

(2)

HENRY THORN was born 1759 in Rhode Island, and was but a babe at the time that his father Isaac was kidnapped, so had no recollection of him. At the age of 16 he enlisted in the Revolutionary Army, taking his bounty money to his mother, who resided in Rhode Island. He joined the army in July, and for seven years he marched and counter-marched from one end to the other of that historic soil until the colonies achieved their independence. He passed the memorable winter with Washington's army at Valley Forge, and was in the battles of Trenton and Monmouth and many others. He was as valorous in love as in war. When peace was declared, he went into service of a rich and aristocratic farmer named Noyes, of Stonington, Conn., and naturally enough, fell in love with Prudence, one of his daughters. The father opposed and forbade their marriage, because the young man was a poor soldier, though admitting that he was of good character, and threatened his daughter with disinheritance if she disobeyed his commands. She married young Thorn, was disinherited and the young couple went to Leydon, Mass., among the first settlers of that town.

Inscriptions on headstones at West Leydon cemetery:
"Henry Thorn, died Oct. 7, 1850, aged 91."
"Prudence (Noyes), wife of Henry Thorn, died Sept. 15, 1840, aged 77. She died full in the faith."

Children: Born in Leydon, Mass.
3 Rebecca, b. 1786; m. Benj. Baker (39)
4 Samuel, b. 1788.
5 Edith, b. 1790, m. Elias Miles.
6 Polly, b. 1792.
7 Prudence, b. 1794; m. Abram Harvey.
8 Henry, b. July 26, 1796; d. March 4, 1885; m. Prudence Miner.
9 Crandall, b. August, 1803; d. Oct. 22, 1878, at Leydon; m. Mary.

HENRY THORN, JR.

(8)

HENRY THORN was born July 26, 1796, at Leydon, Mass. Died there March 4, 1884. He married Prudence, daughter of Jerez Miner of Halifax, Vt. She was born Dec. 28, 1795, at Halifax, Vt. She died Sept. 16, 1851, aged 56 years.

Children: Born at Leydon.
10 Henry Miner, b. Feb. 1, 1821. In 1847 went to Berkshire, N. Y., and married . In 1881 moved to Waverly, where he died March 6, 1884.
11 Roswell M., b. March 1; d. Sept. 13, 1837, aged 13.
12 Isaac N. b. 1823.
13 Eunice. See note below.
14 Rufus.

With the exception of Isaac N., all died earlier than 1886.

Note—Eunice married a Mr. Bullock of Guilford, Vt., and lived at Fitchburg. She died leaving two sons and one daughter. The youngest son was sick and his sister went to Denver, Colo., to take care of him. He died there May 8, 1890, and was taken to Guilford, Vt., for burial by the side of his mother.. They all lived in Pasiac, N. J., where the sons were in the drug business, and the daughter was at the head of the schools of the city.

(9)

CRANDALL THORN was born August, 1803; died Oct. 22, 1878, at Leydon, Mass. Married 1831, Mary Rounds. She was living in Northern Vermont in 1888.

Children:
15 Avery Noyes, d. June 22, 1852, aged 20.
16 Mary, m. Warren Bell in 1888; had one son living, William, aged 13.

ISAAC N. THORN.

(12)

ISAAC N. THORN of Brattleboro, Vt., was born at Leydon, Mass., March 1, 1823; died in Brattleboro, Vt., Jan. 12, 1894, aged nearly 71 years. He was for a long time a widely known and highly esteemed business man. The last years of his life he had been practically confined to his home, though on pleasant days in summtr, he was able to sit in his wheel chair on his veranda and lawn. Rheumatism depriving him entirely of the use of his lower limbs.

Mr. Thorn, having had three or four years' experience as a clerk in country stores in Illinois, Wisconsin and in Colerain, Mass., prior to the summer of 1848, when he came to Brattleboro under the employment of Dutton & Clark, druggists, at the end of ten years, he commenced business for himself and through his reliability as a druggist and his untiring industry he built up a large and profitable business. He had a strong will, won success by his almost resistless energy, was impatient of opposition, but was withal a kind-hearted, honest man.

His first wife, Angeline Augusta, daughter of Cyrus C. Miner, was cousin of Eli W. Miner, who married Mary Baker. She was born May 6, 1832, and died May 27, 1856, at Brattleboro.

His second wife was Elizabeth A. Jackson of Newfane, who survived him.

Children: First wife.
17 Isaac Benton of Brattleboro, druggist.
18 Henry Clinton of Flint, Mich., engineer.
19 Cyrus Edwin of Brattleboro, resides Hinsdale, N. H., druggist.
Children: Second wife.
20 Frank Arthur, a successful physician in Chicago, druggist.

Inscriptions copied from headstones in West Leydon cemetery:
"Henry Thorn, died Oct. 7, 1850, aged 91."

"Prudence, wife of Henry Thorn, died Sept. 15, 1840, aged 77. She died full in the faith."

"Henry Thorn, Jr., born July 26, 1796, died March 4, 1885."

"Prudence, wife of Henry Thorn, Jr., died Sept. 16, 1851, aged 56."

"Crandall Thorn, died Oct. 22, 1878, aged 75 years 2 m:"
Safely across the river, all life's toils and trials o'er,
Sickness, sorrow, pain and anguish, cannot reach that peaceful shore."

"Avery Noyes, son of Crandall and Mary Thorn, died June 22, 1852, aged 20 years."

"Roswell M., son of H. and P. Thorn, died Sept. 13, 1837, aged 13."

Copied from headstone:
"Angeline Augusta, wife of Isaac N. Thorn, born May 6, 1832, died at Brattleboro, Vt., May 27, 1856.

To the memory of a kind companion and an affectionate mother, a bereaved husband has erected this monument."

THE YOUNG FAMILY.

ABIATHER YOUNG was born probably in Connecticut about 1755 and died at Winfield Herkimer County, New York, aged 87 years. He married Lydia French; she was born at Providence, R. I., and died at Wolcott, Wayne County, N. Y., aged 96 years.

But little authentic history has been found concerning this branch of the Young family.

Tradition says that his father was an English soldier, belonged to the navy, and died of yellow fever while on a voyage and was buried at sea.

Another account has it that his father, William Young, came from England, settled in Connecticut, joined the army and was private cab man for General Washington.

We find recorded in town papers of New Hampshire, vol. XIII., page 495: "Abiathar Young, with others in 1781, signed a petition for the incorporation of the town of Wendell, N. H."

On page 499, same volume, relating to Revolutionary service, statement of Captain Samuel Gunnison, dated 1785, to Hon. Committee of Claims of New Hampshire, says that: "Abiathar Young of Wendell, N. H., served in the 'late and unnateral war' one year and nine months." He had just purchased land in the town, made some small improvements and then enlisted in the army.

In the first of the war there were but 22 poles in the town, 15 families, yet the town furnished during the war 19 volunteers.

We find also in the same volume, page 504: Abiathar Young signed a petition May 12, 1791, to have the south end of the town of Wendell, N. H., together with the corners of some other towns, incorporated in another town, and Dec. 27, 1791, the town of Goshen was incorporated.

Children:

Jarvis, d. in Michigan; m. Electa Beach; sons, George and Alexander.
Isaac, had a son, Hamilton.
Asa.
Hiram W., m. Polly ——.
Hezekiah.
Abigail, m. Amasa Howrey.
Sarah, m. Watterman Mowrey.
Mercy, b. Jan. 27, 1807, at Poster, Providence County, Rhode Island, m. Simon Baker.
Lucinda. d. unmarried.

INDEX—BAKER NAMES

The numbers refer to individual records, not to pages, the names being mentioned under the number referred to.

Baker, Abel 21	Elizabeth 13-111-139
Abigail 128	Elizabeth Ann 223
Abraham Coon 184	Elizabeth Orilla 163
Abraham Clain 284½	Emily B. 85
Abner 8	Emma Theressa 167
Agnes Mercy 175	Estella 306
Albert 105	Esther 54-99-242
Alida 144	Esther Emma 223
Albert Edward 311	Ethel 274
Albert I. 153	Eugene 152
Albert Marvin 210	Eunice 71
Albert Mowry 121-181-275	Evaline 234
Alexander Stanley 273	Florence 236
Alexander Steele 177	Florence Genevra 217
Alice 23-213-246	Floyd Earl 310
Alma 216	Frances 104
Amenzo White 120-172	George 22-96-256
Ann 14	George Caleb 207
Annie Leavitt 241	George Lant 289
Annie Maria 212	George Lowell 285
Arva 281	George Washington 123-188
Asa Burdett 277	Gertrude 156
Asa Norman 170	Gideon 113
Ashbel 87	Hamilton Simon 174
Aurilla 78	Hannah 45-75-135
Benjamin 3-18-24-26-39-62-129	Hannah Maria 178
Benjamin George 225	Harold Ray 299
Bennie 224	Hazel May 218
Betsie 122	Hattie 248
Blanche 261	Helen Maria 94
Calvin P. 90	Helen M. 155
Carrie 151	Henry 142
Celestia 196	Horace Curtis 283
Charles 148	Horace F. 81
Charles Duane 278	Howard 269
Charles Henry 183	Hyrum LeRoy 169
Charlotte 130-240	Ichibod 17
Charlotte Annie 179	Increase 57
Charlotte Eleanor 204	Iram 67
Clark 51-95-112	Isabel 159
Clark Arunah 102	Ione 270
Clark Carrington 66	Irvin Lund 276
Clark, E. 154	James 4
Clarissa, E. 149	James Richard 253
Clinton 237	James Staples 138
A child 143	Jane Maria 180
A daughter 19	Jarvis Alexander 161
A daughter 70	Jarvis Young 119
Daniel 20	Jennie 143
David M. 214	Jeremiah 7-136-249
Della M. 157	Jesse 38
Delone 282	Jesse Alvin 291
Doris 297	Jesse Merrit 200
Dorothy Aileen 287	Jesse Simon 186
Earl Morgan 272	Jirah 28-43-49-65-80
Edna 187	Jirah Eaton 58
Edward Orlando 117	John 6-29-106
Elijah 27	John C. 97
Eliza 72	John Daniel 165

John Franklin	303	Mercy	25-31-47-141
John Henry	257	Mercy Rachel	160
John Lyman	290	Merlin Albert	289
John Rupert	202	Mildred	238
John Simon	193	Myrtle	251
Jonathan	52	Nellie	146
Joseph	12-124	Nettie Deloris	288
Joseph Albert	191	Newman	40
Joseph Henry	227	Nina	265
Joseph Linden	199-305	Nina Belle	263
Joshua	11-64	Noah	30
Josiah	10	Noah Chester	171
Julia	190	Norman	36-53-109
Julia Esther	108	Olive	197
Junia	48	Oralia Virginia	286
Laura	185	Osmer	271
Laura Henrietta	293	Percy Jarvis	260
Laura Louisa	254	Philip	15
Laura M.	92	Philetus	91
Lathan	60	Phoebe	132-231-245
LeRoy	250-313	Rebecca	125
LeRoy Pefferle	267	Rena Rachel	264
Leslie	268	Richard Morgan	211
Lottie Margaret	222	Rose	229
Levi	221	Roswell	86
Lois	42	Roxana E.	88
Lola Anona	284	Ruth	259
Lorin Merritt	296	Samuel	59-79
Louie May	294	Samuel Leavitt	134-244
Lucele	279	Sarah	9-34-101-127-233
Lucina	50	Sarah A.	147
Lucy	41	Sarah Ann	137
Lucy Ada	292	Sarah Elizabeth	182
Lucy Agnes	192	Sarah Grace	298
Lucy Amelia	203	Sarah Helen	107
Lucy Louella	301	Sarah Jane	83
Lucy Maria	164	Sarah Margaret	176
Lydia	35	Sarah Sedina	307
Lydia Aurelia	166	Seth	198
Lyman	195	Sherman	33
Mabel	260	Sidney	55-98
Mamie K.	84	Simon	77-131-230
Margaret Edna	219	Simon Clark	44
Margaret Emma	312	Simon Moroni	168
Margaret Pearl	302	Simon Pack	201
Maria	140	Stanley	235
Marquis	89	Stevens	158
Mark	150	Susan	68
Martha	239	Susan Eliza	116
Mary	32-46-56-74-76-100-126-243	Tamson Louella	205
		Thankful	63
Mary A.	82	Thomas	1-2-5-61
Martha Abigail	232	Thomas Edward	308
Mary Agnes	162	Thomas Morgan	209
Mary Ann	226	Thomas Potter	37
Mary Elizabeth	173-208	Vira	252
Mary Emma	189	Walter	262
Mary Esther	93	Ward Eaton	206
Mary Geneva	220	Ward Simon	300
Mary Lovier	295	Wiear	133
Mary Rozina	115	Willard	194
Mary Sibyl	110	William	73-114-258
Maude	304	William Eugene	103
Maurine	309	William Melvin	215
Mehitable	69	Zerilda Jane	113
Melvina E.	253	Zina	247

INDEX—PART ONE

Amos, Rev. Charles 104
Arlington, Edgar 205
   William 188
Atwood, Oralia M. 188
   William 188
   Sarah J. (Wade) 188
Austin, Daniel 14
Babcock, Clark 32
   Lois 26
   Mary 26
   Oliver 26
   Patience 26
Bailargeon, J. A. & Co. 191
Baker (See other list)
Baldwin, Prof 193
Barnes, Alice 181
Barnes, James 181
Barnes, Lydia (Lund) 181
Barrett, Charlotte 250
   Elizabeth Wengren 250
   William 250
Bassett, Sarah 201-202
Barrus, Emmery 118
Beckstead, George 77
Bently, Richard 77
Billings, Geo. 77
Birge, Sarah 43
Bonner, Catherine 64
Boyle, William 149
Brown, James 120
   John, ... 54
Buist, Agnes Burnett 178
   David 178
Burdick, Carey 74
Burton, Col. R. F. 123
Caine, John T. Jr. 193
Canfield, Julia A. 57
Carr, James 101
Chapman, Sarah 52
Chase, John D. 77
Chesebro, Sarah 103
Christensen, Frank R. 190
Clawson, James 77
Clayton, Thomas 77-124
Clive, Prof. U. C. 198
Coney, Enoch 77
Conner, Gen. 121
Coon, Abraham 77-121
   Edna, J. 121
   Elizabeth (Wilson) 121
Cummins, Gov. Alfred 77
Cunningham, Elizabeth 138
   Elizabeth (McBride) 138
   George, ... 138
Curtis, Charles 121
   Jane Maria 121
   Sarah (Wright) 121
Dennett, Isabel 142
Dowdle, Sarah A. 200
   Henriette 200
   Robert 200
Farnsworth, Wm. C. 127

Ferguson, Elijah 63
Field, William 1
Fortier, Prof. Samuel 193
Foster, Lena E. 194
   Margaret (Laird) 194
   Peter 194
Grant, Jedediah M. 77-119
Gibbs, Waity 53
Gifford, Elmira 58
Goatman, George 129
   Lucy 129
Godbe, W. S. 123
Harper, Charles 77
Harrington, Benjamin 34
Harvey, Appleton 121
Hatch H. Sumner 197
Hawley, George 25-31
Haws, Eleeta 133
   Elizabeth (Worsley) 133
   George W. 133
Higgins, Alfred 77
Hill, Archibald 120
   Frances 120
   Jane M. 120
   Janette 120
   John 120
Hinkle, Alice H. 191
Hoephi, Charles 144
Howell, Joseph 193
   William 196
Hulet, Azariah 146
Hunsaker, Abraham 77
Hunter, Isaac 77
Hyde, Orson 77
Jennings, William 77
Jensen, James P. 185
Jens, ... 189
Johnson, Charles A. 192-194
   Claude L. 179
   Joseph A. 176
Jones, Ferris E. 213
Kay, William 77
Kellog, Charles O. 92
Kendall, Thomas 77-124
Kenrick, George 1
Kruyer, Abigail 62
Ladle, Charlotte J. 183
   John 183
   Susanna (Trappett) 183
Lant, Edith 195
Layton, Christopher 77
Leavitt, Abigail (Cole) 77
   Ann E. 134
   Ann E. (Jenkins) 134
   Charlotte 77-121
   Emeline 77
   George 77
   Louisa 77
   Phoebe (Cole) 77
   Thomas R. 134
   Wiear 77
Leishman, Joseph M. 239

Lemon, Charlotte M. (Rawlins)	135
Jasper	135
Mary T.	126-135
Longstroth, William	130
Loomis, Edward	82
Mary	82
Lynds, James L.	242
Mathews, Thomas	128
Matkin, Henry	238
Simpson A.	241
Markley, Christopher	77-123
McCarthy D. & Co.	191
McGary, Major	121
McKelvey, John	83
Miner, Eli	76
Miner, Randall	45
Moffett, Andrew	77
Moore, Samuel	77
Morehouse, Martino & Co.	191
Morgan, Ann (Roberts)	124
Frances A. (Godsel)	177
Margaret O.	177
Margarite M.	177
Mary Alice	124
Owen J.	177
Thomas	124
Morris, Elizabeth	220
Moseley, Arunah	56
Increase	28
Mary	28
Murdock, James	77
Naylor, Thomas	77-124
Neff, Amos	77
Nixon, William	77
Noble, Joseph B.	77
Olds, Dorcas	67
Olsen, Olef A.	240
Ormsby, Dr. O. C.	188
Owens, David T.	204
Pack, John	124
Lucy A.	124
Lucy (Ives)	124
Patterson, Dinah (Stanhope)	44
Eleaser	44
Roxana	44
Pefferle, Pauline	161
Pete (Indian)	121
Perry, H. C.	124
Potter, Mary	24
Pratt, Lola	184
Lorus	184
Owen W.	184
Zina (Wheeler)	184
Preston, William B.	121
Price, William	77-125
Raybold, A. W.	203
Reeves, Col. John	77
Richards, Agnes	123
Agnes (Hill)	119
John	119
Rachel	119
Rollo, Randolph B.	147
Rowe, Elizabeth (Murdock)	129
Margaret A.	129
William	129
Self, Samuel H.	222
Seipons, Amasa	85
Sessions, Peregreen	77
Scribner, Samuel	35
Shelp, S. V.	191
Shepardson, William H.	46
Sherman, Elisha	24
Mary	24
Shumway, A. P.	123
Spencer D.	139
Smith, Prof. Joseph F.	198
Reuben	84
Snow, William	77
Sorensen, Abraham	174
Christina	174
Spencer, Samuel G.	180
Staines, Elder	77
Staples, Ann	77
Elizabeth	77
James	77
Louisa	77
Louisa (Field)	77
Richard	77
Sarah (Limerick)	
Steele, Agnes	120
Alexander	120
Jane (Martin)	120
Stillman Samuel N.	119
Stone, Merlin J.	138-140
Stringham, Bryant	77
Sweet, Stephen	14
William	1
Sweeten, Prof. R. L.	193
Taylor, Mary R. (Shoulders)	62
Thomas	62
Tanner, Mary	37
Terry, George	69
Thomas, George	193
Thorn, Henry	39
Prudence (Noyes)	39
Rebecca	39
Topham, John	77-124
Tucker, Hannah	26
Twist, George	77-124
Vaughn, William	1
Walker, John	77
Walker Bros.	191
Webster, Ellen M.	221
Emma (Cleg)	221
Samuel	221
Waters, Edwin	75
Welch, Lucina	51
Wells, Daniel H.	124
Wright & Sons, W. H.	191
Young, Abiathar	77
Brigham, Sr.	119-121-123
Brigham, Jr.	77-124
Lydia (French)	77
Wescott, Amos	4
Deborah (Stafford)	4
Penelope	4
Wheeler, John G.	184
Willie, Elizabeth	121
William	135

INDEX—PART TWO

Adams, Charles 368
Arlington, Edgar 205
   Joseph B. 492
Arrowsmith, James L. 663
   James T. 419
Baker, Mercy R. 160
   Elizabeth O. 163
   Lucy M. 164
   Sarah E. 182
   Edna 187
Barton, S. S. 368
Bird Alice (Stokes(..... 379-381
   Taylor 379-381
Brown, Emily A. 339
   Fannie M. 549
   F. Leone 550
   John 54
   Jonathan 337
   Lucina 334
   Mary 335
   Miner 352
   Sarah 338
   Sarah (Miner) 352
   Susan 336
Buist, Annie A. 448
   Earl A. 449
   David 178
Boyle, Carrie 438
   Charlie 439
   Edith 441
   Emma 436
   Estella 442
   Harriet 440
   Lorin 435
   Mabel 442
   Mary 437
   William 140
Burdict, Ann J. 347
   Caleb 346
   Carey 74
   Jackson 348
   Jesse 349
   Oscar 345
Butler, Betsie Jane 561
   Caroline (Farozine) 367
   Caroline M. 562
   Charlotte E. 558
   Ernest H. 563
   James 367
   James A. 559
   John T. 560
   John L. 367
Christensen, Andrew 190
   Corinne 473
   Florence 475
   Franklin 474
   Franklin R. 190
   George 476
   Marion (Williamson) 190
Clark, Albert 620
   Charles 389
   Grace 621

Evans, Alice 657
   Charlotte 655
   George W. 658
   John W. 405
   Phoebe 656
Eyre, John 368
Farnsworth, Euclid 388
   Grace 389
   William C. 127
Farr, Atherton 467
   Lucien C. 467
   Sarah (Holden) 467
Ferguson, Elijah 63
   Ira 344
   James 342
   Mary 343
Granger, Anna M. 401
   Leva T. 401
   William W. 401
Graham, George 599
   Ida M. 680
   James 599
   Jane (Laird) 599
Harrington, Benjamin 31
   Cyrus 314
   Sally (Avery) 311
   Sidney 521
Harvey, Emma (Foerhand) 598
   Harold L. 679
   Robert 598
   Robert B. 598
   Robert W. 677
Hastings, Floyd L. 674
   George E. 667
   Harold H. 675
   Keneth W. 672
   Lillian M. 670
   Leon S. 666
   Leon V. 681
   Mabel E. 668
   Mattie L. 676
   Raymond M. 669
   Robert F. 671
   William S. 522
   William W. 673
Hatch, Hezakiah E. 197
   H. Sumner 197
   Georgia (Thatcher) 197
Hoephi, Charles 144
   Rudolph 443
   Willie 432
   Winfield 434
Hogensen Bodel (Monson) 166
   Helen Aurelia 446
   James C. 166
   Melba Doloris 445
   Neils 166
Horsley, Ernest S. 368
   Samuel P. 368
   Sarah (Barrows) 368

Howell, Joseph 196
   Mary E. (Maughan) 196
   Spencer B. 484
   William R. 483
Hubbell, Emma 533
   Missouri 532
Hawkins, Gladys ....R. 617
   Glenn M. 618
   Michael 383
   Elizabeth (McNulty) 383
   Solomon M. 383
Jensen, Agnes 468
   Albert Rex 46½
   Christina 185
   Edna 464
   Esther 470
   James P. 185
   Jens 189
   Karen 189
   Laura LaRue 462
   Lillian 469
   Mabel 460
   Mary 467
   Mary (Mortensen) 377
   Milton 471
   Olive 472
   Peter M. 377
   Peter R. 461
   Royal B. 463
   Sibyl 465
   Victor 466
Johnson; Albert M. 381
   Alice I. 601
   Andra 619
   Avice H. 479
   Alice M. 612
   Charles A. 192
   Charles H. 480
   Claude L. 385
   Cora D. 606
   Cora M. 383
   Dorrit A. 613
   Fern A. 615
   George W. 192
   Gladys L. 478
   Ida M. 598
   Irma P. 481
   Joseph A. 382
   Joseph R. 482
   Juanita I. 477
   Kenneth B. 616
   Kieth, T. 610
   Lorna A. 609
   Maggie 603
   Minnie 602
   Miriam S. 192
   Marion N. 378
   Murl I. 611
   Mercy L. 386
   Norman D. 607
   Nancy (Greer) 125
   Orel M. 599
   Orville W. 608
   Orville D. 384
   Rebecca L. 600

   Snellen M. 125-604
   Taylor R. 605
   Thomas I. 379-597
   William W. 380
   Willis 125
   Zelda M. 614
Jones, Ferris E. 213
   Ferris J. 493
   Joseph L. 494
Kellog, Charles 365
   Charles O. 92
   Christina 364
   Frank 364
   Mary L. 364
Kenedy, James C. 531
   Roy 531
Leishman, Ellen B. 507
   Ellen (McKay) 239
   Idonna 511
   Joseph Mc. 239
   Leroy 509
   LeVern 508
   Robert 239
   Samuel 510
Lambert, Asabel 532
   Calvin 536
   Celia M. 535
   Elizabeth (Shepardson) 333
   Elsie 541
   James L. 332
   Janette 538
   Lester W. 533
   Lewis 539
   Mary E. 534
   Walter 540
   William H. 537
Larson, Guy 639
   Mary 637
   Miles 640
   Vera 638
   Peter 400
   Theodore 641
Longstroth, Alice 408
   Alma 409
   Charlotte A. 400
   Clara M. (Sorensen) 407
   Ethel 410
   George S. 403
   Lyman 411
   Mary 402
   Phoebe 405
   Phillis 660
   Rosetta 404
   Sarah 406
   Stephen 401
   William 130
   William G. 407
Loomis, J. Edward 82
   Jeffie 354
   Jennie 353
   Josie Hoyt 354
   Hoyt 551
Lynds, Ida M. (McNult) 242
   James L. 242
   John E. 242

Maddox, Benj. F. ... 420
   Frederick S. ... 420
   Perenial C. (Clark) ... 420
   Ruth E. ... 664
   Viola C. ... 665
Manning, Alfred ... 651
   Blanche ... 652
   Emily ... 650
   Emily (Wilson) ... 404
   Frederick C. ... 404
   Frederick J. ... 404
   Hugh ... 653
   Louisa ... 654
Mathews, Abie ... 634
   Annie (Gray) ... 394
   Bessie ... 635
   Bessie (Ence) ... 398
   Carlton ... 632
   Charlotte A. ... 395
   Earl ... 633
   Elizabeth (Lawrence) ... 399
   Elsie ... 628
   Frank ... 631
   Frank W. ... 622
   Francis M. ... 396
   Joseph S. ... 398
   Lester ... 625
   Littie L. ... 630
   Mary M. ... 397
   Maud ... 623
   Roy ... 399
   Sarah ... 629
   Sarah (Williams) ... 396
   Thomas ... 128-624
   Thomas W. ... 394
   Vera ... 636
Matkin, Bert B. ... 501
   Elmer B. ... 517
   Gladys ... 503
   Harold ... 505
   Hazel ... 520
   Henry W. ... 238
   Lois ... 502
   Lottie M. ... 519
   Mildred ... 504
   Muriel ... 506
   Samuel ... 238
   Sarah (Wilkes) ... 238
   Simpson A. ... 241
   Vivian B. ... 518
   William Henry ... 500
Merritt, Grace ... 667
   John ... 534
Miner, Alton J. ... 525
   Angie L. ... 524
   Arlou R. ... 526
   Austin W. ... 318
   Benjamin R. ... 316
   Caroline L. (Brown) ... 325
   Eli W. ... 76
   Ellen ... 327
   Emeline ... 326
   Emily ... 319
   Jerrah C. ... 325

   Laurinda ... 315
   Leon J. ... 523
   Lucy ... 322
   Lydia S. ... 323
   Marilla ... 317
   M. Genevra ... 522
   Norman B. ... 320
   Randall ... 45
   Sarah ... 352
   Sibyl ... 324
   Silas ... 321
Moseley, Arunah ... 56
   Jirah ... 340
   Mary ... 341
   Sarah (Shapeley) ... 56
Muir, Armaid R. ... 648
   Byron L. ... 646
   Grace ... 647
   Hazel ... 643
   Jane ... 402
   Maggie ... 642
   Melvin T. ... 644
   Stephen L. ... 649
   Thomas ... 402
   William G. ... 645
McKelvey, Byron ... 355
   John ... 83
Nyman, Carl A. ... 162
   Carl B. ... 444
Olsen, Albert ... 240
   Annie ... 200-513
   Elsie ... 512
   Elsie (Benson) ... 240
   Keneth A. ... 515
   Olef A. ... 240
   Samuel A. ... 516
   Oliver ... 514
Olsinger, Wm. ... 549
Owen, Alta Tanzen ... 488
   Belle ... 491
   Charlotte ... 490
   David F. ... 204
   Ethel M. ... 487
   Grace E. ... 489
Parsons, Alice ... 527
   Elmer Y. ... 528
   Clara ... 529
   Jonah M. ... 329
   Mary (Shepardson) ... 329
Peterborg, Alfred T. ... 408
   Theodore L. ... 661
Pof. Rev. W. A. ... 45
Rathbun, Chas. E. ... 88-555
   C. Eugene ... 361
   Frank A. ... 363
   Harvey V. ... 557
   Laura ... 556
   Wm. E. ... 362
Raybold, Albert W. ... 203
   Doris A. ... 485
   Lynn W. ... 486
Reynolds, Elizabeth A. (Norton) ... 375
   Josiah ... 375

Robinson, John 373
  John O. 589
  Jane (Coop) 373
  R. A. 368
  Susan M. 588
  Thomas 373
  Thomas A. 587
Ross, Laura J. 340
Self, Bertha M. 495
  Henry I. 496
  James Merlin 497
  Laura A. 499
  Mabel P. 498
  Margaret A. (Craven) 222
  Samuel H. 222
Shepardson, Desire 521
  Jane (Felch) 330
  Joseph 330
  Lucinda 331
  Lydia E. 333
  Maria 531
  Mary 329
  Salome R. 332
  Sophia 530
  Thomas J. 521
  W. H. 328
Shumway, Alvord L. 662
  Andrew 421
  Annie L. (Willis) 417
  Bradford P. 422
  Charles 139
  Henrietta 419
  Henrietta (Bird) 139
  James Melvin 426
  Lettia M. 424
  Lydia 418
  Merlin 423
  Sarah E. 420
  Spencer B. 417
  Spencer D. 139
  Zina 425
Smith, Augustus A. 359
  A. D. 222
  Clement 465
  Emily C. 356
  Frances (Vanoy) 465
  Frank 358
  Fred 554
  Mary M. 357
  Reuben 84
  Thomas 465
  Willie 360
  Geo. A. 122
Sorensen, Frederick C. 447
  Frederick J. 167
  Jacob 167
  Susan (Hancock) 167
Spencer, Albert B. 450
  Alma 451
  Charles 459
  Clawson 454
  Daniel 180
  David 452
  Mary J. (Cutliffe) 180
  Owen 457

  Pearl 453
  Rhoda 453
  Ruth 458
  Samuel G. 180
  Zina 456
Stone, Bertha M. 428
  Daisy L. 427
  E. Maude 429
  Merlin J. 140-430
  Mabel E. 431
  Daniel 368
Taylor, Maud 626
  Miles 627
  Miles R. 395
Thomas, W. N. 179
Topham, Alice E. 569
  Alice (Robinson) 370
  Amelia (Jenson) 377
  Angus R. 586
  Annie E. 581
  Annie M. (Nielson) 371
  Asa E. 568
  Bertha E. 579
  Betsie J. 570
  Clara E. 567
  Charlotte E. 367
  Eulala 592
  Geo. A. 372-582
  Harriet I. 594
  Harriet I. (Reynolds) 375
  Hyrum S. 376
  Ina L. 576
  James 366
  Jane (Thornton) 122
  Jesse W. 566
  John 564
  John B. 365
  Joseph E. 584
  John C. 573
  John K. 580
  Joseph L. 574
  Joseph R. 375-590
  Laura A. 583
  Laura E. (Horsley) 372
  Lucinda (Robinson) 370
  Margaret E. 575
  Mary J. 577
  Mary J. (Smith) 369
  Mercy J. 368-572
  Merlin June 593
  Rulon J. 596
  Sanford M. 595
  Sarah L. 585
  Silas M. 594
  Silas S. 377
  Simon T. 370-571
  Stephen 565
  Susan A. 372
  Thomas A. 371-578
  William 374
Townsend, Henry 380
  Nellie (Seales) 380
VanWormer, H. S. 353
Waters, Amanda 351
  Edwin 75-350

Webster, Carlos 350
   Frank 239-553
   Mollie 552
Whiting, Arthur W..................................545
   Edwin 347
   Ella J. 544
   Emma L. 542
   Francis L. 347
   Francis Lester 548
   Lucia L. 543
   Mary B. 546
   Sylvia C. 547
Willie, Charlotte 414
   Elizabeth 135
   George 413
   James G. 135
   James S. 412
   Maude 415
   Sarah 416
   William P. 135
Wintle, John W..................................427
   Joseph B. 427
   Mary M. (Wilson)..................................427
Wright, A. R...................................406
   Lucy C. 659
   Lucy (Wardrop) 406
   James W. 406

Milton Keynes UK
Ingram Content Group UK Ltd.
UKHW021835240124
436635UK00007B/570